WINTER AT LONG LAKE

www.allnationspress.com
All Nations Press
P.O. Box 601
White Marsh, VA 23183

Winter At Long Lake: A Childhood Christmas Memoir
ISBN 0-9725110-9-1

Manufactured in the United States
First Edition

Winter At Long Lake

A Childhood Christmas Memoir

By

Rick Skwiot

All Nations Press

To Romana Swann,
who showed me the way home.

Some of the names have been changed
— by faulty memory or design.

...I, on my side, require of every writer, first or last, a simple and sincere account of his own life, and not merely what he has heard of other men's lives; some such account as he would send to his kindred from a distant land; for if he has lived sincerely, it must have been in a distant land to me.

—Henry David Thoreau, *Walden*

...The lake stretched away and away into the distance. This expanse of water was an inconceivable pleasure to me, an incomparable splendor. At that time the idea became fixed in my mind that I must live near a lake; without water, I thought, nobody could live at all.

—C.G. Jung, *Memories, Dreams, Reflections*

Foreword

I'll tell this story as best I can, but it happened so long ago that it comes to me as a fable, something vivid yet remote. And it seems even more distant because so much has changed so quickly, so much has been lost, irretrievably.

For me that change began here, on Long Lake, at Christmas 1953. Nothing that happened after that day carried the same solid spirit that had imbued life before then, not for years. But eventually I found that the spirit of that place—the feeling of solid earth, hushed peace, and hard love—might, with great effort, be retrieved, even if the place itself and its time are gone forever.

I see it now, vague, distorted, mysterious, as if glimpsed through a window iced with morning frost.

Christmas Eve

I

Translucent glass. Morning light waking me on the back porch, where I insist on sleeping even in coldest weather. The sun refracts through Jack Frost scroll-work painted on storm windows that replaced summer screens, those covered during hot thunderstorms by a beige tarp nailed to a beanpole and lowered on ropes.

I lie in my narrow bed, peeking out from layered blankets covering me, studying patterns on the glass. There on the sill a sweet-potato plant and a carrot grow from two jelly jars I keep filled with water, now topped with ice.

My robe—brown wool plaid with white twine belt—lies on the foot of the bed. I manage to turn and worm my way under the blankets to it and pull the cold robe into my warm burrow. I get my arms into the sleeves, tie the belt tight, and rise with the blankets wound round me Indian-style. My stockinged feet find wool-lined slippers resting on the frigid floor. I shuffle to the far end of the boxcar-sized room where an iron stove sits.

There I kneel, open the coil-latched door, and peer inside to find dim coal ash on the iron grate. As I shake the grate by its metal handle, gray ash sifts below revealing glowing orange coals. From a galvanized bucket to my right I feed fresh coal into the stove with a black tin shovel until the bucket is empty.

I sit before the open door of the warming stove on a rustic, unpainted chair that my father made me for my sixth birthday the previous February along with a child-sized workbench that mimics my father's. Beneath the blanket I exchange my robe and blue flannel pajamas for my uniform: long cotton underwear and argyle socks; brown cord trousers with difficult button fly and rabbit's foot dangling by a brass chain from a belt loop; a hand-me-down cloth Boy Scout belt; oxblood combat boots, so-called, with laces and buckles; home-sewn gray flannel shirt; green sweater with reindeer.

I carry the blanket, pajamas, and slippers back to my rollaway bed. From a low peg by the kitchen door I take a maroon gabardine coat, mittens clipped to its sleeves, and fleece-lined bombardier's cap, worn in four seasons.

Coal bucket and tin shovel in hand, I push out the back door into a still cold that stings my face, careful not to let the screen-door slam and wake my parents and big brother, who sleep within the house. Though it really isn't a house. Just an old fishing shack on the banks of a long-dead branch of the Mississippi, a summer clubhouse, as they are called, which my family has made into a year-round home. Let them sleep, I think, while I stoke the stoves so they can wake to a warm house.

A cardinal sitting on the faded white picket-fence that guards the steep lakeshore catches my attention by singing: "Cheer, cheer, cheer." As I move toward the garage, hard-frozen Illinois bottomland crunching beneath my boots, I look up to the tall plum tree just on the other side of the fence, where a blue jay squawks out a warning.

In the blue sky behind the jay a silver airplane lit iridescent by morning sun crosses east to west. I see four motors turning propellers but cannot distinguish any markings to determine whether it is a Red bomber come to level our home or simply an airliner taking holiday travelers across the river to St. Louis. But the plane passes over without incident.

Moving onto the gravel drive I veer away from the chicken-wire pen where the old black man shot and killed my father's hunting hound. As much as I love animals, I am glad the dog is gone, and still avoid the pen as if its ghost lurked there.

Sam, as my father named the dog, was no good except with his master. On winter mornings, when frost crisscrossed the tall grass and illuminated the dead weeds along the fields of black earth as the first sun hit, my father would go out to the pen with his double-barrel shotgun broken in the crook of his arm, leash Sam, and head out walking cross the furrows in search of rabbit or quail. Sam had short white hair with rust-colored splotches and thin, pink lips. Father wore a beige canvas hunting-coat with red shotgun shells fitted in canvas holders on the belt.

When beside my father the dog would only whimper and never bark unless he sniffed a rabbit or bird. But if anyone else came near Sam's pen—the chickenwire sides eight-feet-high to keep the animal caged—he would bark, snarl, and show yellow teeth that made your heart race.

One day when the metal hinges on the gate of his pen pulled out of rotted wood, Sam got loose and chased my brother, Eddie, crying inside the house. Next week when the colored men came with their truck to cart away the trash that wouldn't burn and the garbage that didn't get buried, my mother told me to go inside and stay away from the windows. When I asked why, she said that she and my father had decided Sam had to be put away. Then she took the double-barrel shotgun from the closet where Father kept it and carried it outside.

Peering out the slit of the raised bathroom window I saw my mother give the gun to the older Negro, who tipped back his worn felt hat, put one shell into the gun, and snapped it shut. The sound came to me like a door being locked. Then the man walked over to where Sam stood snapping at him inside the repaired pen and lifted the gun to his shoulder. The gun jerked back, shaking the old black man's spare body. The explosion echoed across the lake and the dog dropped silent to the earth. Then Mother turned back to watch the men throw Sam into the truck with the trash and move down the drive.

Now I circle the empty dog pen looking across the cracked white corn stalks and withered bean plants still clinging to their poles and see something that stops me cold. Where the smelly cabbages grew, the door on a rabbit-trap has swung down. The coal bucket slides from my hand to the hard ground, the shovel clanging inside it, and I run to the garden. Then I slow to approach the homemade trap, not knowing for sure what I might find inside.

Dropping to all fours on the ice-crusted earth, I bend to peer through the wire mesh on the far end of the wooden box. Beyond the peg that held the apple that tempted him sits a fat, brown rabbit, fear-eyed and trembling. I stare back, reaching my right mitten under my coat to touch the severed rabbit's foot dangling from my belt, knowing the animal will likely be on the table tonight. A ripple of hot awe passes through me as I contemplate the rabbit's death and my own good luck in having rabbit to eat. But I do not know that my luck, like the rabbit's, will soon turn dark.

At the garage I stand on tiptoe to raise the metal latch that keeps the two great wooden doors—white paint grayed and cracking—from swinging open on their hinges. I block one door closed with a rock and let the other glide open a few feet, enough for me to pass inside with the coal bucket.

Backed into the dark garage sits a black prewar Plymouth smelling of grease and rubber. I move around the creased front fender where Father slid the car into an icy bridge coming home from the night shift at the steel mill in Granite City, and then pulled out the dent by hooking the fender to the big maple in the front yard with a chain and backing up, tires spinning and smoking in the grass.

By gray morning light I find the coal bin door and pull it open. With the tin shovel I fill the bucket resting on the gravel floor, black dust rising earthy to my nose. Using both hands I lug the coal past the Plymouth and back toward the house, clouds of warm breath hanging before me in the still air and settling damp onto the false-fur collar of my coat.

Inside I doff the coat and carry the coal through the dark kitchen and into the living room, where another stove sits cold. I steal over the worn carpet, place the coal beside the stove, and kneel to open the door and shake the grate. Making as little noise as possible, I load coal into the stove and shut the iron door. I rise to put an ear first to the door of my parents' bedroom then to that of my brother but hear no one stirring.

As I turn back, my eyes fix on the Christmas tree

standing tall and dark in the corner, its unlit star on top nearly touching the ceiling. On it hang strings of popcorn laced on waxed thread, chains of red and green construction-paper strips glued with flour paste, gingerbread men adorned with white icing buttons and raisin eyes (all of which I helped make), scant store-bought ornaments, and meager strands of colored electric lights that go black every time one bulb blows. As I kneel before it, the green fragrance of balsam resin comes to me. I gaze at a fragile globe of silver glass hanging by a mere thread, a precarious little world afloat in black space. In the ornament I see a distorted reflection of my own face, eyes oversized, as if my dominant feature.

I focus next on the manger beneath the lowest branch. The scene of the infant Jesus, Joseph, and Mary surrounded by animals in the still night fills me with a sense of warm well-being. I lie on my stomach under the tree, gazing at the family secure in the manger...

*

At least that's how I remember the day beginning. Though, except for the Christmas tree, it might have been most any winter morning. For those were always the rituals of sunrise: reviving the fire, checking the traps, hauling the coal. Later that Christmas Eve as the sun climbs and falls there will be other rituals that shape the day and help shape the year—and shape me as well.

II

At the kitchen table I sit before a bowl of Cream of Wheat studying the picture of Captain Midnight on the Ovaltine jar, feeling a mistake has been made. This man looks nothing like he sounds on radio.

My mother, who was next to rise, pours herself a cup of coffee from the percolator on the range and adds a dollop of canned milk before sipping. She stands fair-haired and tall—nearly as tall as my father—in a navy wool skirt, gray pullover, and red apron, looking out the window over the sink.

She has the radio tuned to The Breakfast Club. When they play the daily recorded march she likes to lead me marching around the kitchen table. But not today. It is still too early for the march, and the radio voices drone softly as her husband and older son still sleep.

She sets down her cup. From a wooden box in the cupboard she counts out six small potatoes dug from the garden and scrubs them with a hard bristle brush in the sink. As she works she stares out the window past the sandbox her husband built for their two sons and across a field of amber weeds to the frozen lake.

Perhaps she is thinking back to warm summer nights when she paddled our leaky blue boat across the still lake, my brother and me seated on the wooden floor-slats bailing out water with tin cans and, at the front of the boat, the soft-green line of my father's fly rod undulating in the dusky sky. Or maybe she is simply enjoying the austere winter landscape—gray skies, gray iced lake, gray-beige fields. Or planning what she must do for Christmas dinner at her mother's, for in the refrigerator a goose awaits the oven. Or maybe she's remembering the shotgun flat in the city where they first lived and where the landlady downstairs scolded Eddie, then just three, for digging in the backyard. Probably not the last, since a faint smile comes to her pale blue eyes, as if she's savoring a fond memory or anticipating a pleasure, and she hums along to "God Rest Ye Merry, Gentleman" now lilting low from the radio.

Breakfast potatoes washed, she dries her hands on her apron and cuts from a pan on the kitchen counter a square of the German butter-cake her mother taught her to make. As she takes a bite her eyes again are drawn outside. A squat, cream-colored truck with red script on its side has stopped at the Suttons' house a furlong up the road. She turns to see me finishing my cereal and sings: "Milkman!"

I look up to her wide-eyed, reminding her perhaps of photographs of her husband as a child: the same dark eyes, full lips, and round face, coffee-colored hair brushed to the side.

"Can I?"

"Yes, you may. Have you finished your cereal? Okay, go on."

But as I push up from the table and go for my coat she has an afterthought and waves me to her. "Come here, Rickey. Let's give you some of this."

From the kitchen counter she takes a bottle of cod-liver oil and pulls a tablespoon from the drawer. I stand by, dutifully awaiting my dose. I watch as she pours the translucent yellow-green liquid onto the spoon. The aroma makes me wrinkle my nose, but I can't decide whether or not I detest its taste and wonder if, like beer, it's something bitter one comes to savor.

After retrieving my cap and coat from the peg I bolt for the back door.

"Don't forget the bottles," my mother calls after me.

I let the storm door slap closed behind me on its long spring.

When the Massey Dairy truck pulls up I am waiting at the end of the gravel drive beneath the sign my father made. "Lazy Lane," it reads, silver on black, with a varnished picture cut from a magazine-cover of a bass breaking water. The driver looks down through the open door to me holding the empty milk bottles. I stand ready, eager to leap into the truck. Since I started first grade in September, I have not ridden with Bill.

"Want to ride with me, Rickey?"

"Can I?"

He waves me in. "Come on."

The truck will make six stops before it reaches the dead-end a mile down the black tar road and turns around. At the first driveway I ask if I can carry the metal basket of white milk bottles to the door and fetch the empties. Bill strokes his chin.

"I reckon it's okay." But then he adds: "You're not after my job, are you?"

"Oh, no sir."

"Go ahead then. But be careful with it."

From the first house I bring back two empty quart-bottles and a note, which I hold before me, and announce: "Two quarts eggnog."

Bill moves into the back of the truck, which in summer drips water from its melting ice steaming onto hot tar. But today everything is frozen solid—the earth, the lake, the ice in the truck. He reappears with a cream-colored bottle in either hand.

"Where'd you learn to read like that?"

"I'm in first grade now."

Six times the truck stops and six times I run up with the usual order and retrieve empty milk bottles. Four times I run back with special orders—eggnog, extra milk, more butter or cream—because of the holiday.

The road ends at a furrowed field of broken corn stalks. I come running back down the drive from the

Nolan's house, eyeing the spot where Charlie Washburn got run over. Bill reverses the truck then heads it back up the road.

He drives standing up, the long black-knobbed shift-lever between us. Sharp winter air blows through the open door where I stand.

"You cold? Want to close the door?"

I shake my head. The wind numbs my face as I look at the dead fields flowing past. I see a covey of quail shoot from brown roadside weeds, feel the morning sun break through thick clouds and come warm through the windshield to mix with the cold wind, and hear the truck-engine's roar, feel it vibrate through my boots on the cold metal floor and into my bones. I sense Bill's eyes on me, look up, and return his smile.

I know it is good. Good to have the wind in your face, the feeling of movement, and fertile fields all around you. But I do not fathom how truly good it is, nor how tenuous.

III

I come through the back door to the aroma of onions and bacon frying. As I remove my coat I hear my father's voice.

"Maybe something closer will turn up."

"It's a good opportunity, Ed."

"I'm not sure it's right. Besides, it won't go away."

"But it's been two months now."

"I know how long it's been."

When my father sees me standing in the kitchen doorway, a wide smile comes to his dark, lank face. His voice, deep and resonant, calls out:

"There's my little soldier. Come over here."

I point toward the window as I approach. "R-r-rabbit," I stutter, as I do when excited.

"Where's the r-r-rabbit?" says my father, wrapping me in his arms and pressing coarse black whiskers into my cheek.

The smell of my father—man scent and tobacco—comes to me. My mother and the other women I know smell like roses or lilac, but the men—my father and his friends who come from the city to hunt and fish—each have a distinct animal smell that I could distinguish blindfolded. I answer:

25

"The trap in the garden. Can we get him?"

"After breakfast. Then we'll get him and skin him," he says, running his fingers up my ribs. He calls to my mother, "What do you say, Veta? Hasenpfeffer tonight?"

She does not turn to respond but speaks looking out the window to the gray fields. "Wash your hands," she says, which brings my brother running into the room.

I dig into my meal. The salty bacon comes from the farmer with the bad-smelling sty at the crossroads, the orange-yolked eggs from the Suttons' dark hen-house, where the fearsome spurred cock roams the yard and, screeching, chases me. The potatoes and onions come from our own garden, the bread from dough my mother has kneaded and baked, the plum jelly from the tree by the lake.

My father asks us what we learned in school the previous day. Eddie tells about his fourth-grade Christmas program, which I had witnessed, where he played the old toy-maker who falls asleep and whose dolls and toy soldiers come to life, singing, dancing, and reciting poems. When it's my turn I shrug.

"Nothing."

"What do you mean 'nothing'? Didn't you pay attention?"

"Yes, sir."

"Well, what did you do?"

"Reading and addition and drawing Christmas trees. But I knew that already."

My father leans back raising black eyebrows. "If they can't teach you anything there, maybe you're ready for college." He turns to my mother. "What do you think, Veta? Should we send him away to college next year?"

The thought of being taken from my home, my lake, and my family leaves me speechless. I study my father's face to see whether he is earnest.

"Don't tease him, Ed. No, Son, we won't send you away."

My father goes on: "Well, maybe you're not ready for college. But you must have learned something there by now."

I think, trying to remember what might have been new to me. Then I strike upon it: "Atom bomb drill."

My father shakes his head. "Is that where you put your head between your legs and kiss your..."

"Ed!"

"No, we go away from the windows and sit under our desks and put our arms over our heads like this."

"That's good. That's real good. I'm glad to see my boys are getting an education."

My father drains off his coffee and says: "Who's ready for rabbit?"

I slide off my chair to run for my coat and cap. My

father turns to my brother and tousles his blond hair.

"Don't you want to help?"

Eddie winces behind eyeglasses, shakes his head, and moves off to the front room to play with the electric train under the Christmas tree, a train that my father—who never had a train as a boy—bought him for his first Christmas nine years earlier.

My father and I pace together across the frozen garden, his hand resting on my shoulder. At the cabbage patch we sit on our haunches side by side. He hooks the hinged door of the rabbit trap and sets it on end to study the animal inside.

"He's a big one," he says.

He carries the trap to the garage and retrieves from his workbench red rubber gloves, an iron bar, and a hunting knife in a leather sheath. Then back outside to the gate in the picket fence and down wooden stairs to the boat dock, me following. On the shore near the dock stands a sturdy but crude homemade table stained with blood and littered with fish scales. He sets the trap on the table, pulls on the rubber gloves, and releases the hook on the door.

I fix my eyes on my father's hand as it reaches in and pulls out the rabbit by the scruff of its neck.

"Want to pet him?"

I pull off my mitten, nodding. I reach up to where the rabbit sits on the bench and stroke its back, feeling its flesh quiver beneath the warm fur.

Then my father takes the iron bar in his right glove and taps the creature's neck at the base of the skull. It falls limp on the table. He unsheathes the hunting knife and makes incisions around the neck and up the stomach. With the red rubber gloves he reaches inside to pull out blue and purple guts, organs, veins. I hear the sound of rubber squishing in blood, and a raw fecal stench comes to me.

Holding the animal by the head, my father skins the rabbit bare, cuts off its feet and head, and then carries the rabbit and the offal to the lakeshore. He kneels and, using the iron bar, cracks a hole in the ice. He washes the carcass in lake water and lays it stretched on the ice.

I stand transfixed over the red flesh of the animal, staring at its lean haunches and recalling the sharp taste of marinated rabbit and vinegary sauce spooned over mashed potatoes.

My father pushes the innards and the rest into the opening, washes the rubber gloves there, and removes them.

"Want to skate?"

At the sound of my father's voice I look up from the blood-red rabbit.

"Can you pull me?"

"Okay. Take these things to the garage and put them where they belong. Then get your sled. But stay at the

29

shore till I'm back."

We move together up the wooden stairs to the picket fence. As my father disappears inside the house with the rabbit, I carry the rubber gloves, iron bar, and hunting knife into the garage. I return them to their proper places and retrieve a sled of worn brown wood and black steel hanging from a nail on the west wall of the garage, my father's boyhood sled but now my own. Careful not to let its runners scratch the black Plymouth, I carry it out into the daylight and down the stairs to the lake.

The lake looks more like a river than a lake—and once was. It sits on the American Bottom, the wide Mississippi flood plain. And although the Mississippi now lies twelve miles distant, some claim this once was a channel of that great river, perhaps thousands of years ago. But the river changed course and left behind this dead river called Long Lake, which runs from Mitchell five miles southeast to Pontoon Beach and Horseshoe Lake, and is only a hundred yards wide on average. The same Indians who built the giant Monks' Mound a few miles south also built mounds along Long Lake.

The first Europeans to come to Long Lake were French trappers, who found forests of walnut, elm, hickory, oak, and cottonwood; great prairies; and ample wild game—deer, rabbit, turkey, bear. But the first permanent white settler on Long Lake was James Gillham, who came upon the area while searching for his wife and children, who in 1790 were abducted by Indians from his Kentucky farm. After five years he found them at a Kickapoo village on Salt Creek, near present-day Springfield, Illinois. After ransoming them he eventually settled his family on Long Lake, whose grassy prairies, fertile black earth, abundant timber, and pure water had impressed him. I love it too. It seems abundant to me as well.

My father has not yet returned from the house so, lying belly-down on the sled, I push myself along the ice near the shore, pressing my wool mittens against the leaf-ridden ice and lunging forward. I move away from the dock, eyes trained on the ice passing beneath me, sliding out from the shore to where the ice lies smooth, and the going gets better. Then a black image flashes past. I drag my boots to stop, roll off onto the ice, and scurry back on all fours to it.

There, a half-foot below the surface in clear, rigid water, lies a black cat with white boots—the Suttons' missing cat Boots, her last breath now bubbles captured in ice. I lie on my stomach gazing at the creature trapped within the hard lake, imagining its creeping unawares over thin ice, falling through to the frigid water, and struggling vainly to free itself. I lie on the ice as if frozen, staring, puffs of white breath hovering over me in still air.

I hear a footfall and turn to see my father coming

down the wooden stairs to the lake with ice skates tied over his shoulder. I retreat toward the shore where I was ordered to remain. Walking ahead of my sled, pulling it by a clothesline tied to its frame, I approach my father, who sits on the boat dock lacing up his skates.

He wears a wool cap, burgundy letter jacket, and gray wool socks with a red band at the top, into which he tucks his charcoal-gray trousers. A cigarette hangs from the corner of his mouth, the good-smelling smoke wafting to me. He lifts the cap from his head, smoothes back his straight, black, widow's-peaked hair, and places a hand on my shoulder. Without a word he tosses his cigarette aside hissing on the ice, rises, and glides off across the lake, skates clanking against the ice then cutting an arc on it when he turns.

I watch his trim figure moving over the lake as if pulled along by an invisible hand, like a leaf blown across the sun-lit ice. Now he returns, racing toward the dock, coming faster and faster. My heart quickens. I'm afraid he won't be able to stop in time and will crash into the wooden pier. But at the last instant he turns his skates to the side and shushes to a stop, sending a spray of shaved ice into my face.

Squinting and smiling, I brush the ice from my eyes.

"Hop on and let's go." His voice comes to me higher and lighter than usual.

Lying flat on the sled's slats, chin touching the cold

metal frame, mittens clutching the wooden steering bar, I look up to him and nod. "Okay."

Its taut pull-rope in my father's hand, the sled begins to rumble across the lake. His skates glint in momentary sun and pound the ice. Soon the sled is skimming the lake, me hugging it like a lifesaver, my father bent forward, legs straining.

A quarter-mile down the lake we begin a wide turn. I feel the centrifugal force urging me from the sled and hook my ankles in the runners. Now the sled is moving sideways, too. I glance up to my father with a mix of fear and exhilaration as the far lake-bank approaches, trying to see if he recognizes the danger and can keep the sled from plowing into the thick-trunked cottonwoods there. The bank comes closer and closer, the trees come faster and faster. Then suddenly the sled lurches forward and skirts the shore as we complete the turn and move on a line back home.

Ice kicked from my father's skates blows stinging into my face. The slick shining surface slips by beneath. The sound of metal on ice comes to me muffled by my earflaps.

"Faster!" I call, "Faster!" and imagine the day I will skate there beside him.

But that day will never come. This December day with my father and me gliding over the frozen lake in tandem is the last time I remember seeing him move so gracefully.

IV

As the train rounds the bend, white smoke billow-
ing from its stack and steel wheels churning, the crossing gate at the gray-painted road drops, bells clanging.
Lying on my stomach on a braided rug my mother made
from scraps of cloth, eyes at ground level, I imagine
the cardboard village real, place myself at the throttle
of the locomotive, and feel its power vibrating through
my fingertips on the train board. When the train passes
by my eyes, my brother leans forward at my father's
urging and presses a red button on the control box.
The train whistle mourns, and I start.

"Ed..."

My mother, still in her apron, stands in the doorway of the front room wiping her hands on a flour-
sack dishcloth. My father brings the train to a halt and
turns to her:

"Come on, Hon. Your turn to sit on my lap and
blow the whistle."

She shakes her head at him the same way she does
when I spill my milk.

"I'm out of vanilla. Would you run up to Sis's for
some? Take the boys with you." Without waiting for a
reply she retreats to the kitchen.

Eddie says, "I'll stay and play with the train."

"You'll get your coat on and come with me. Your mother needs some peace and quiet."

I have already jumped to my feet and am racing through the kitchen for my coat and cap. I know that my brother is wasting his breath. There seems to exist between my parents a secret treaty that bars open disagreement on any matter, however trivial.

Besides, now I am eager to get out of the house. My mother naps on the sofa every afternoon and it is far better to be out of the house for whatever reason than be forced to sit quietly inside it while she sleeps. Or, worse yet, to lie still beside her cradled in her arm as I did before starting school.

Outside I unlatch the garage doors and prop them open with two large white rocks placed at either side of the structure. A bank of low gray clouds comes to obliterate the sun, and a gust of wind sways the bare branches of a weeping willow by the driveway. I lower the fleece earflaps on my cap and button them together beneath my chin. My father comes out the back door of the house—its facade of fake beige-brick peeling in spots to reveal black tarpaper beneath—his arm lying across my brother's shoulders.

My brother and I sit side-by-side on the worn, gray-wool front seat of the Plymouth as my father grinds the starter. Finally the motor kicks to life with a shud-

der. He puts it in gear and lets out the clutch pedal. We move from the dark garage into the dim day.

Once off the gravel drive and heading down the straight, flat, black-tar road that cuts through fields of black earth, Eddie asks if he can drive. My father lifts him onto his lap. He takes the wheel, feet dangling toward the rubber-mat floor. As we pass the Sutton place we spy Dickie chopping wood beside the henhouse.

"Give him the horn," my father says.

When it sounds, Dickie looks up and waves.

A mile further, as we come to a crossroads where a gray tarpaper building sits beneath signs for Red Label Beer and Orange Crush Soda, the car slows. Eddie cranks the big black steering wheel hard left and moves the car onto the potted gravel lot.

I run inside first and am greeted by the familiar and comforting smell of stale beer, an aroma I associate with laughter, music, and being put to bed in a wooden booth, a coat as my blanket. The slat-floor room lies dark and shadowy in the glow of jukebox lights and electric beer-signs, including one above the bar in which a silver-blue stream flows perpetually through pine-covered hills. On the bar sits a small, tinseled Christmas tree, and I haul myself onto a barstool there.

As my father pulls the thick door closed behind him, a thin, gray-haired woman with rimless glasses emerges

from the back room. She moves behind the bar, reaches across, and touches my cheek as I study the wrapped packages under the tree.

"Merry Christmas, Rickey. Santa came early, and I think he left something for you and your big brother."

She reaches for one of the packages and hands it to me.

"Thank you, Miss Sis."

"Well, open it."

I tear off the printed paper and inside find a red Hauptmann cigar tin filled with homemade cookies. My brother takes a sugar cookie to the bowling machine and pretends to play but has no money for it.

As my father sits at the bar drinking beer from a brown bottle, the woman moves to the adjoining confectionery and returns with a small brown vial of vanilla. She sets it on the bar and slides a dime across to me.

"Play us some Christmas music, Rickey."

As I move to the jukebox by the door I hear Sis say, "Any word from the mill, Ed?"

I dawdle there as if deciding what to play but in fact trying to comprehend the conversation behind me, which I know is not meant for my ears. I hear my father's voice:

"There's nothing coming in. I think it's finished, Sis."

The dime makes a hollow tinkling sound as it falls through the machine. I select "Frosty the Snowman," "Here Comes Santa Claus," and "Silent Night." Then I

go to the bar where Sis serves me a root beer. I turn away pretending to watch my brother at the bowling machine, where he slides the heavy metal puck monotonously up and down.

"No chance of getting called back next year?"

"Not without World War III."

"What will you do, Ed?"

There's a silence, and I picture my father drinking from his beer bottle and raising his black eyebrows. Then I hear the bottle knock once on the wooden bar.

"Veta wants me to take a job selling insurance in St. Louis. The fellow who sold us my life policy said I was well spoken. Just right for it. But I've always worked with my hands. And there's the house. We've put a lot of work into it in six years. I'd hate to leave it."

I feel something on the back of my neck like a cold breath and stare up at the lighted sign with the flowing stream. Leave my home. The thought is so startling, so alien, that I cannot grasp it. How could my family possibly abandon our garden, our lake, our rabbits? How could we not live where we belong—how could we not live at home?

Suddenly the Christmas music, the sugar cookie I nibble, and the syrupy drink lose their flavor and come to me too rich and sweet, and for a moment I fear I will be sick.

V

The used Plymouth sedan comes with aromas. I inhale them as we drive back from the tavern: the wool of its seats, the rubber of the floor mats, a greasy smell coming from beneath the metal dash. Then, as I snuggle next to him on the front seat, my father's scent, a beer, tobacco, and man smell.

When I see my father's foot depress the worn clutch pedal, I shift the car into third gear. He takes the old lake road home, steering around potholes that came after the snowstorm two weeks earlier. The holes will grow larger and deeper until June, when the yellow road-grader comes like a giant grasshopper spitting out broken tar and releasing a pungent aroma of oil and dirt into hot summer air. Two days later the hulking, beetle-like tank-truck arrives spewing black liquid, followed by a dump-truck losing beige gravel from its tail-gate. For days my father must leave the car at the crossroads and walk home along the weedy ditches that border the road. Then, when he finally brings the car home again and turns up the grassy drive, beige gravel sticks to the tar-splattered running boards. But now the road is a slick, pitted black ribbon.

The Plymouth suddenly slows and turns onto a

white gravel drive with grass growing between the stones. I look to my father, who answers my tacit question.

"Your mother needs some time alone. We'll hang out here for a while. See how Cal's doing."

The car halts beside a small, white-slat house on the lake, and my father gives the horn two quick toots. The air outside feels not much colder than that inside the Plymouth. The three of us move around the back of the house and through a door onto the screened porch, enclosed now with storm windows. My father knocks at a heavier door with peeling white paint.

I know this house, the home of Calvin Miller, with whom I sometimes play. But I come visiting with mixed emotions. For although Calvin is always ready for most anything—to sneak out onto the ice, to chase rabbits on the farmer's land, to climb tall trees—his mother is always afraid for him and ever watchful. Maybe because of what happened to his father.

She comes to the door wiping her hands on her apron. A wiry, black-haired woman, she looks old to me, older than my own apple-cheeked mother. She smiles with sad, watery eyes.

"Well, Merry Christmas, Ed. Isn't this a surprise."

We step into an overheated room where Cal Senior is sitting up straight in his wheelchair, grinning and straining to see who it is, like a dog anticipating its dinner. He has gray-black hair, a gaunt, weathered face,

and bushy, black eyebrows. Calvin Junior is sitting on the oval rag carpet beneath a wooden lamp with horseshoes on its shade, playing with miniature plastic cowboys.

I feel my father's hand in the middle of my back pushing me forward toward the man in the wheelchair. I go to him reluctantly, for a smell hangs about him that is not the pleasant man-scent of my father but a stale, musty aroma of old blankets and wet newspaper, a smell of death and decay. The gleaming metal chair in which he sits seems forbidding and potentially infectious to me, like something from a hospital cellar. But I go to him and endure his hands on my head and face, then turn to the television before which the crippled man sits.

Cal nods toward the screen and says to my father:

"Christmas on the 38th parallel. Some of the same boys from my old unit, poor bastards. At least we were warm when we fought the Japs."

No one talks much about World War II. I know that my father did not go but instead worked at the steel mill making tanks. Others, like my Uncle Harry, went and came back with German daggers and flags.

My eyes return to the wavering images on the small, circular television screen. I see lines of tired-looking American troops, their breaths visible, marching up a dirt road among tanks, jeeps, and trucks with white-painted stars on their sides. A man's voice comes speak-

ing of Seoul and the July armistice. It is the first TV set I have seen except for ones in store windows downtown, where people crowd to watch the World Series. I understand it is a good thing for a man in a wheelchair, who cannot ice-skate.

The woman says to her son:

"Calvin, why don't you boys go outside for some fresh air. But stay off the lake."

Calvin Junior fetches his coat—just like mine, with fake fur collar and belt that closes with a metal clasp, but gray instead of burgundy.

After the hot living room, the outside air cools my face. Calvin says:

"What do you guys want to do? Shoot marbles?"

"Too cold," says Eddie.

"Cowboys?"

I shake my head. "Army."

Among the trees on the bank that drops to the frozen lake we find fallen branches that serve as rifles. We then move stealthily through the woods down to the shore to ambush Chinese Communists attacking across the ice from North Korea. Calvin is wounded in his left leg when he charges out bravely but foolishly smack into the Commie guns, and I wonder if his father did the same against the Japs.

Though I sometime fear that the airplanes crossing high above the Illinois plain may be Communist bomb-

ers, I have been reassured that their troops and tanks will not come up the road to threaten us. I cannot imagine such a thing happening except in make-believe, nor can I imagine going overseas to kill Japs or Communists. I do not wish to leave my peaceful home for any reason.

But still war is all around me. Born a year-and-a-half after the end of World War II, but three-years-old when the Korean War begins, and surrounded by those for whom war is a fresh and vivid memory, I am steeped in war.

From the radio I have heard of Inchon, Pusan, and Panmunjom. And although my mother will not take me to war movies, she does permit me comic books of G.I.s killing Reds. And I listen, always listen, for stories and hear my parents and their friends speak of ration cards, victory gardens, draft boards, and artillery castings. Among the men I listen for tales of battles—of shooting Nazis and bombarding Japs—for I know they have such stories. But I never hear any. Most other boys have gas masks, bayonets, or army caps that their fathers brought back from the war, but their fathers never speak of what happened there. Robby Nolan, who lives at the dead end of the lake road, has a phonograph in his room and plays for me songs about firebombing Herr Schicklegruber and making the Japs into chop suey. Also I have learned that the Braden

sisters, teenagers who live with their mother near the crossroads, had a father who went missing in the war.

I play make-believe war and dress like a soldier, tucking my brown cord trousers into my combat boots. I have even created a make-believe hero, Gunson Boots—a name inspired by Puss in Boots—whose identity I adopt when playing soldier. I also have a set of miniature plastic soldiers with tiny tanks and artillery that my uncle gave me the previous Christmas.

But despite all the artifacts and ghosts of war lingering about me, and the TV images that brought it to mind on this day, its force pales when compared to that of the Wild West. Cowboys, Indians, and the open range have long dominated my play and my daydreams.

Only recently have I outgrown the cowboy boots handed down from my brother. Also now too small for me is the black Hopalong Cassidy costume that was my Christmas present two years earlier. Nonetheless it is easy enough to dress up like a cowboy, with checked, snap-button shirt like Roy Rogers', red neckerchief, high-crowned cowboy hat, and black-holstered six-shooter cap gun. And to imagine my chestnut stallion with the pure-white blaze beneath me as I gallop across cornfields transformed into desert canyons. Or, on hot summer days, to remove my shirt and wear the red neckerchief as an Apache headband to good effect (for by July I am darker than most movie Indians), hunting

buffalo with the bow and arrows I make from saplings on the lake bank.

My brother identifies, unaccountably, with Gene Autry, the most unmanly and girly-voiced of the movie cowboys. I prefer Lash LaRue and Whip Wilson, whom I see in serials at the Lincoln Theater in Granite City on hot Sunday nights, who dress in black, and who inspire me to fashion a bull whip from my father's old belts.

But the play, like the bloodless cowboy movies themselves, is generally non-violent, with more cattle rustling, hiding out, and horseplay than gunplay and scalping. Besides, the cap guns are often broken. Or the red-paper strips with dots of explosive somehow get twisted and misfire. Or I don't have two cents for caps. Or my brother explodes what few caps remain with a hammer while I'm at the lake. Then the two Matayas sisters, Janet and Marleen, come down the road dressed as cowgirls, wanting to play a more genteel and domesticated form of cowboys, with homesteads, working ranches, and square-dancing.

But for all the material trappings of cap guns, cowboy hats, homemade bows, and Indian teepees, the Wild West most captivates and invigorates me due to something I sense deep inside. I feel it when Hopalong intervenes to save the poor rancher from bandits, when Roy and the boys sit around the campfire singing of Old Mexico, and when the heroine streaks across the

mesa on her pinto, her long blonde hair buffeted by the wind. It is a feeling of justice, of camaraderie, of life without fences, for which, like most boys, I always long.

VI

The scents of the stewing rabbit and the Christmas tree, the warmth of the coal stove and the fragrant kitchen, the feel of my father's rough beard and muscled arms, the cheer of the Christmas-tree lights and the toy train whistle, please my senses and my soul. But after a time this comforting yet largely inactive day begins to tire me. The air inside the house hangs still and suffocating. I sit alone and listless at the kitchen table playing solitaire mechanically. The good, free feeling I had that morning when I flew over the frost-touched earth in the milk truck with December wind in my face has vanished, thanks in part to the conversation I overheard in the tavern.

This is the only home I have known or ever wanted to know. I've seen other homes and how others live— on the narrow brick streets of my grandmothers' neighborhood in St. Louis, or in the new, treeless, landlocked suburbs where my parents' friends have fled the city. I love my shimmering lake, black fields, fruit trees, birdsong, and hedges hiding rabbits. I love the dead-still nights, rough blankets, and heavy coal buckets; the icy winters, the sweltering summers, and the solitude. I cannot bear the thought of losing it all.

The sun hangs low in the sky behind gray clouds visible through the kitchen window. Soon it will be dark and I will be trapped inside for the long evening. So to escape my thoughts I don my coat and bombardier's cap—though without great enthusiasm—and head for the back door.

"Don't go on the lake," my mother warns.

"Yes, ma'am."

When I step through the door the cold slaps my face, and I am suddenly invigorated. Weather, always the weather. And the seasons. They dictate everything. The work you do in the garden, the games you play, the foods you eat, the clothes you wear. Whether you fish or hunt. Even your moods.

In winter there's checking the traps, chasing rabbits, and playing hockey on the frozen lake—a chaotic affair with skateless boys banging a tuna tin across the ice with tree branches, sliding and falling on slick-soled shoes, wrestling and laughing. There are snow forts and snowball battles and long nights listening to the radio, playing checkers, drawing pictures, connecting the dots, ogling seed catalogs, baking cakes, and making popcorn.

With spring comes the furrowing and planting and kites made of willow branches and tissue. There's digging worms, searching the lake for awakening fish, climbing trees to see baby robins chirping in fear, and watching for tulips to reappear, for apple trees to blossom pink

and white, for the first corn-shoots to break the earth.

The long summer is filled with weeding, hoeing, and harvesting the fruits and vegetables as they come ready: the lettuces, strawberries, cucumbers, and melons; the peas, beans, corn, and potatoes; the cherries, peaches, and apples. Off come shirts and shoes.

Going shirtless, like Tarzan, is a manly thing to do, and all the boys do so as do most girls—at least until they start first grade and are made to feel self-conscious. In the family photo-album is a snapshot of me, my brother, and half the Sutton brood under the maple tree by the lake on a summer day, all shirtless, grinning, and sun-darkened, with hair shorn helter-skelter, resembling restive apes more than civilized human beings.

None of the boys up and down the road and across the fields—with the exception of the Nazarene preacher's son—wear shoes in summer, either. You can run faster without them, wade right into the lake, and feel the grass, warm earth, and mud between your toes. The only look-outs are for snakes, sharp rocks, and, when you have to cross the black-tar road on hot, hot, high sun days, the tar that sticks to your feet and raises blisters.

On such days I'll return home shirtless and shoeless for the evening meal, coated with dirt and dust, looking like I've been rolled in cinnamon. My mother shakes her head then soaks me in a galvanized washtub in the backyard where I transform clear water into weak tea.

But it's hard to stay clean when you're playing King-of-the-Hill on the dusty lake bank, eating watermelon and ripe plums, digging worms, raking the muddy shoreline for crawfish, or lounging on the dock with your cane pole waiting for the cork to bob. Also there is Indian Ball, where you catch a batted ball then throw it at a bat on the ground to win a turn at hitting. And Statues, where you have to hold a pose after being twirled around and released; Red Rover, where you try to break through a line of kids linking arms; Mother May I, in which you must remember to ask permission before taking giant steps or scissor steps; and dodge ball, which teachers call Elimination but kids call Lemonade. You also shoot off firecrackers when your parents aren't looking and sit in the shady backyard sipping green Kool-Aid and playing cards. Some days you dig the Panama Canal in the sandbox and fill it with lake water and wooden boats fashioned from scrap lumber, then jump in yourself. Or you lie under the sycamores looking for four-leaf-clovers in the grass or lumbering animals in puffy thunderheads sliding high over the flatland. You swing on the long branches of weeping willows and make whips of them to tame your tiger-brother. Evenings you sit on the slat floor of the flat-end rowboat, sit leaning against your mother's knees as she paddles you quietly over the black-glass lake. Your father's fly line cuts a soft, hissing S in the dusk and the stillness breaks with a

silver splash as a bass leaps to shake the fly from its lip.

In fall I rake leaves and jump in the soft yet scratchy pile, roast marshmallows over a fire on the shore, and help with canning the vegetables, washing the storm windows, preparing for the coming cold. One day while I rake golden maple and brown sycamore leaves into a bed, I hear screams coming from the lake. I run to the fence to see Wayne in the bow of a boat holding out his hand, a bloody red mass.

"Pancho shot me! Pancho shot me!" he cries.

And this is not like the blood of rabbits or sunfish, nor the make-believe blood of dead soldiers and Indians. I feel a tingle in my groin and a rock in my chest and run inside to my parents.

But make-believe comes in all seasons. Make-believe cowboys and Indians, make-believe war, make-believe weddings when the Matayas sisters come to play. There are make-believe pirates, cops and robbers, knights and tyrants; make-believe mountain climbing, parachute jumping, and auto-racing. All with make-believe dialog, make-believe scenes, and make-believe plots that create make-believe emotions that sometimes seem as good as real.

In all seasons there are tag, hide-and-seek, and marbles. Especially marbles. We play rounds, where you draw a circle in the dust and gamble your worst marbles at its center, shooting knuckles-down from the circle's edge to win them back and add others to the cloth pouch you carry on your belt. We also play holes, where you dig a baseball diamond in the piebald back-yard and shoot your marbles from base to base to home. Yet marbles are not just plain marbles, but aggies and cat's-eyes, steelies and swirls. Marble playing is to the neighborhood boys what baseball is to America: a largely passive pastime with gambling and occasional brawls.

I play marbles even in winter, on the worn front-room carpet with my father and brother, drawing a white chalk circle on the brown wool and forever trying to beat my father. But I never can, and he knows better than to let me win at this, at checkers, or at cards—that's part of the code, and a good and necessary part, for it keeps me striving. My mother does not much care about the chalk circle on her carpet and will try to sweep it away the next day with the old, mechanical carpet sweeper. But she has to wait for a week's wear before the circle disappears.

We likely cannot afford a vacuum cleaner or do not think it necessary. (We also either can't afford or don't need a TV, telephone, or electric toaster.) Nonetheless my mother—likely out of passivity or boredom—al-lows an Electrolux salesman to give a demonstration one evening. He comes with his great gleaming ma-chine and a dozen attachments and begins to vacuum the old brown carpet. Miraculously, it starts turning beige before our eyes.

"See! See!" the salesman cries.

My family huddles on the sofa, silent and aghast, watching the machine pulling up the dark brown threads one-by-one and exposing the beige backing, sucking our carpet away. But we all are too embarrassed to say a word to stop him. Afterward my mother makes a braided rug to cover the bare patch, like a bad toupee on a bald spot.

But now on this late December afternoon I pull on my mittens against the quiet cold and breathe it into my chest. No wind moves through the naked plum, maple, and willow trees that stand guard beyond the picket fence at the top of the lake bank. A blue jay squawks then quiets, and all is still.

Later in life I will become accommodated somewhat to the incessant growl of traffic, the sound of sirens in the night, the buzz of telephones, the hum of air conditioners, and the crescendos of jets passing overhead, all the background noise of city life that eventually retreats halfway into your subconscious, like a mild toothache. But here and now, as the jay concludes his say, perfect silence lies. No car on the road, no airplane above, no wind, no nothing. Then the sound of my boots on the frozen earth and the whisper of my gabardine coat as my arms swing in short arcs.

I move past the old, landlocked boat that my father

hauled from the lake bottom, ratcheted up the bank, and deposited by the sandbox. From its bow I have plied vivid seas defeating tyrants, vanquishing evil buccaneers, and rescuing fair maidens. I know that as a man I will in fact face tyrants, evil, and maids in distress, but do not yet realize how daunting such real-life confrontations can be.

The picket fence ends at the propane tank, beyond which lies a fallow field of head-high weeds through which I have tromped a maze with dead-ends, secret rooms, and foxholes. The last accomplished with the folding army-surplus shovel I asked for and received from Santa last Christmas. With it I am forever digging—digging for worms to bait my hook, digging furrows to plant seeds and seedlings, digging for arrowheads and buried treasure. The waiting earth holds such gifts, and I know that if I dig deep enough I will surely find them.

But as I steal through my maze I hear the bark of a dog. Then distant cries. I race through the tall brown weeds and out the other side. There, across the shorn wheat field, I see the Suttons moving with their dog Tippy.

I run to join them. The band contains three of six brothers—Russell who's in second grade, Roger in fourth, and Dickie in fifth—and their five-year-old tomboy sister, Patti. They move in a pack, sticks and rocks clenched in their fists, following Tippy, who sniffs the ground in front of him.

When they see me Russell calls: "Get yuns a rock, Rickey. We're for rabbit."

I run to the road pulling off my mittens, find two hefty stones in the ditch, and join the tribe.

Soon Tippy pauses and sniffs under bushes at a drainage ditch running to the lake. We stand tense, expectant. Then a scuffling sound in the dry leaves, a bark, and the blur of a rabbit shooting past our legs. The chase is on.

The beige rabbit zigzags across the rough field. Tippy lays back his ears and leads. We hunters race behind, loping over furrows, puffing, Patti's long brown locks bouncing on her shoulders. My heart pounds in my neck. My hands perspire round the rocks clutched there. Cold air whistles in my ears.

We follow the black dog and the white tail of the rabbit moving crazy across the field toward the road. There it drops into the parallel ditch. I run with the others on the shoulder of the black-oil road, our shoes pounding the earth with a rasping rhythm and throwing up bits of brown rock, moving together, yelping like Tippy, cold air grating our lungs. Then our quarry disappears into a culvert beneath a farmer's road. We race to the other end, but the rabbit does not come.

We stand huffing, then kneel at either end of the tin tube to spy the animal shaking within. Tippy barks at the far end. Our band of hunters waits at the near end, weapons poised. But the rabbit does not move.

With our sticks we bang on the tin. Still the rabbit will not budge. Then Russell thinks to light dry leaves with the discarded lighter he carries and shove them into the culvert with his stick.

Now, with the smoking leaves and barking dog at one end, the rabbit bolts from the other, where our band waits. Rocks fly, clubs beat the earth. The rabbit circles within our cordon and suddenly flies twisting in the air as a rock catches him. Dickie moves in with his club, aiming for the animal's head, to kill it cleanly and quickly and keep the meat intact. Once, twice his stick falls, and the rabbit lies still, light brown fur on the dark brown earth, bright red blood on the fur. Russell holds Tippy back as we bend to examine the animal and to stroke it.

The Suttons carry it off to their roadhouse home and the dinner table. I watch them retreat with it, stand still watching them walk tight together with their game dangling from Dickie's hand. Then I hurry home, happy now for the warm stove and hot meal that await, for the sun setting orange over the fields, and for the story I have to tell.

VII

Today, Christmas Eve, is a school holiday and I am thankful for it. For I have been able to glide across the lake with my father, play soldiers with my brother, and run in the fields chasing rabbits instead of facing confinement in the classroom.

Already after just some four months of school I have become bored. I detest having to sit quietly at my desk for most of the day, and pass countless hours gazing out the window at the wind-waved wheat and drawing wooded, blue-water crayon landscapes. I also hate marching in line, playing organized games under adult supervision, and feeling that at any time I might innocently break some secret rule and be sent to the scowling, red-faced principal, Mr. Lee, and his electric paddle.

It seems so odd to me to have this rigid institution of cold brown brick set in the countryside where, in September, farm kids come to school barefoot and, in a wheat field just behind the school on the shores of Long Lake, lie thousand-year-old Mississippian Indian mounds. It sits like a citadel at the far end of the lake, in Mitchell, Illinois, where Route 66 crosses the railroad tracks and great trucks roar by. My father has taught me how to signal the drivers to sound their air horns, with a gesture like pulling the streetcar cord when it's your stop. At recess and lunchtime I stand at the chain-link fence guarding the highway, making this gesture and feeling the startling sound of the horns and the rumble of the trucks vibrate through me.

Despite that pleasure, there are few good and forti-fying things about the place—the most noticeable exception being my teacher, Miss Bush.

Unlike most teachers at Mitchell School, she never lays a hand on a child in anger and seldom sends any-one to Mr. Lee. Facing the flag for the Pledge of Alle-giance each morning, she stands tall and ramrod straight, hand held hovering over her heart, silver hair fixed flaw-lessly atop her head, suit pressed, embroidered linen handkerchief tucked into her sleeve. An exacting but patient and kindly woman with a love for drawing, she creates wonderfully correct colored-chalk orioles, blue jays, and robins on the blackboard and makes perfectly round O's and Q's beneath the painted alphabet that runs above it.

Each day while the other students do addition she sits in the back of the room with the new boy, a bare-foot Mexican, teaching him to count to five on an aba-cus. And one day she takes me aside out of earshot of the others and shows me how to speak slowly, distinctly, and thoughtfully, so I will not stutter so.

When, after only a few weeks of school, time comes

for my first report card, I pull the thick folded card from its manila envelope. But there are no grades, only elegant but incomprehensible writing on the bias in the feared cursive. Though I can make out the printed page just fine, handwriting seems like Arabic to me, and knowing that I will have to tackle it in second grade fills me with dread.

But two things help accommodate me to school.

One is the fondness I develop for the tools of my trade: the resiliency and rubbery aroma of my eraser; the fine feel of chalk dust on my fingers; the variously colored boxed crayons in neat, soldierly rows; the curled filigree shavings when I sharpen my bright-yellow pencil; the rough, pale-yellow, blue-lined sheets of my Big Chief notebook that smell of the woods; the thick-and-thin dancing lines of serifed F's, G's, and question marks in my texts; and the authoritative spell of words printed in black ink on grained stock.

Second, there is the magic allure of the worlds within those books. Without discouraging my daydreaming nor my love of drawing pastoral scenes, Miss Bush guides me to the small library beneath the windows by the wheat field, where she has deposited adventure books, biographies of great Americans, ancient fables, and old texts. From there I read children's stories of pirates and soldiers, of Lincoln and Edison, and, most entrancingly, of the Plains Indians who roamed the same flatlands as me. This last in a fifty-year-old first grade reader, an unadorned brown-cloth book with mesmerizing pen-and-ink drawings of Kickapoo, Kaskaskia, Illiniwek, and Sioux roasting game at their hunters' campfires, spearing fish from rivers and streams, passing icy winter nights in caves and lean-tos. Here, I feel, are true kin, these hunters and braves. As I read of their trials I reach to the rabbit's foot dangling from my belt and pray to be that kind of man, a brave.

Then there is a third unexpected though, for the time being, less compelling schooldays intrigue: girls. I experience my first infatuation, in a rather mild way, with a dark-haired beauty named, exotically, Lana, as well as my first deep recognition of the special otherness of girls. I already knew that girls were different: They dressed differently and played with dolls instead of guns and marbles. But now, as a first-grader, I have come to feel that difference in the pit of my stomach. These are special creatures who free feelings of excitement in me that no boy ever could, not even my best friend Ethan. I notice this when Lana, who sits in front of me, kneels on her chair and leans forward to help a classmate with subtraction, and I glimpse her white cotton underpants beneath her starched dress.

In addition to her long, shiny black hair, what draws me toward Lana is her worldly status as an older woman. She had been sick much of the previous year and now has to repeat first grade. She has been vague about the nature of her illness, but I accept as truth that she had been sick, for serious illness among children is not unusual. Penicillin is still rather new. Tuberculosis tests and polio vaccines have recently come into use, although too late for Toni, a classmate who ambles about stiff-legged on metal braces, and Robert with his withered arm.

In October I take home a paper for my parents to sign granting their permission for the school to inject me with polio vaccine. Then one day without warning or further prelude I am marched onto a school bus and carted ten miles into Granite City to another school. There I stand in line watching my classmates' arms being pierced with a long needle, one after another, by a man in a white coat seated on a wooden stool. As the line shortens and I move closer, I see the needle disappear time and again into fleshy little arms. I feel myself growing faint, for my experience with needles and doctors has not been good.

Once, when I was three and suffering a high fever, my parents took me into town to the office of Dr. Koch, a smiling woman in another white coat. While attempting to inject me with medicine, she broke the needle off in my buttock and needed her surgical instruments to retrieve it. The mishap greatly amused my father. For weeks he repeated the story of his "tough-assed son" to bartenders, neighbors, and perfect strangers. But

I was not amused, and the sight of the needle repeatedly puncturing those ahead in line makes me want to bolt. But I don't. As always, I stand and take my medicine.

Similarly, my class is once paraded onto the gymnasium stage where a team of dentists stuff cotton balls and metal clamps into each child's mouth and spray our teeth with a foul-tasting concoction said to be fluoride. When I ask my father why I have to endure this, he just shrugs.

I submit to these manhandlings with a passivity born of the respect for school authorities demanded by my parents, whose own staunch authority I cross only at great peril, both physical and psychological. For my father's wrath and my mother's tears are fearsome each in their own way.

The school authorities also use fear as an effective disciplinary tool. Teachers routinely tell students that the unkempt and off-limits cemetery adjacent to the playground contains quicksand that will swallow up a child, and point to half-sunken graves as proof. Although these warnings don't scare me enough to keep me from sneaking away from my classmates during recess and into the grassy graveyard, I do so carrying a stick, tapping the earth in front of me like a blind man. Likewise, despite Miss Bush's admonitions to avoid the "slop ditch" (a rank open sewer that runs between the school property and the wheat field behind it) and its poisonous serpents, I have never seen anything there more dangerous than a garter snake.

The inhibiting legend of Mr. Lee's electric paddle has also been let grow, passed on from class to class. Some older boys even claim to have survived it and thus draw great respect from first-graders. From such accounts I picture the device as a riverboat paddlewheel turned on its side, a Gatling gun of corporal punishment designed to make you cry. The folklore of the electric paddle is made even more plausible by the forbidding demeanor of Mr. Lee, who roams the hallways wild-eyed and snarling, looking like a demented tent-preacher (which perhaps, on Sundays, he is), hair parted down the middle, taking long, straight-legged strides, never smiling except for a feline grin that is all mouth and no eyes, like a cat ready to devour a mouse. He is obviously a heartless man capable of most anything, and I can easily imagine him at the control panel of the electric paddle laughing diabolically.

Additionally, most teachers—excepting Miss Bush—keep paddles prominently displayed in their classrooms. It is one of these—the unsmiling second-grade teacher Mrs. Tate—who sets off my father's battle with the school when she grabs me in the hallway as I cartwheel past her door and spanks me with her weapon of choice, a slat paddle in which she has drilled a hun-

drink. But most of the kids have never seen a baseball game and so swing the bat like they are chopping wood and run the bases clockwise.

Once, after Mr. Gage sends us back to our classroom near the end of the day, I linger and, from behind a stout maple, study him, a towering and broad-shouldered man of perhaps thirty, with a pockmarked face. He ambles to his dented black Chevrolet sedan and promptly backs it into the tree where I hide. Then he steers it forward into the brick wall that guards the incinerator. Once again putting the car in reverse, he turns to spy me peeking from behind the tree. He gestures for me to return to my classroom, then holds his index finger to his lips to signal silence. This is our secret, and I keep it secret until now, until its telling can do him no harm. That too is part of the code.

VIII

I sit at the round oak table hands folded, head bowed, my father to my left, my mother to my right. My brother, seated across from me, leads us in the ritual prayer that asks Jesus to dine with us and bless our food. Eyeing the plate of steaming rabbit in the center of the table as I pray, I remember it trembling in the rabbit trap just that morning and slip my hand beneath the table to touch my rabbit's foot.

Death and sacrifice are a natural part of my life: big fish eating little fish, robins eating worms, bats eating mosquitoes. But killing—whether rabbit, fish, fowl, or crawdads—comes only from necessity, to eat or use as bait. Or, in the case of snakes and mosquitoes, to keep from being eaten yourself. This too is part of the unwritten code, though my brother once broke it by killing robins with his BB-gun. It is something you just know: Killing without good reason or torturing animals, even snakes, is wrong and will sooner or later bring bad luck. All us boys know this just as we know to fight fair, work together, share our food, and not sass or act mean. We know how to hunt as a band, how to choose our leaders, and how to settle disputes. We know this just as we know to eat when hungry, rest when tired, and honor our own family first.

The hasenpfeffer comes in a dark, vinegary sauce that goes on the mashed potatoes. We also eat canned green beans from the garden, homemade bread, and, for dessert, the long-awaited Christmas cookies. These I helped my mother make weeks earlier, mixing dough, cutting tree- and bell-shaped sugar-cookies before sprinkling on red and green colored-sugar, dressing gingerbread men with raisin buttons and white-icing belts, and licking clean spoons and bowls. Then I stood by ready to sample each batch as it came hot from the sweet-smelling oven. But since that evening the cookies have been off-limits and out of reach in tins on the highest pantry shelf.

After dinner I help my mother with the dishes, kneeling on the kitchen-stool to reach the sink, where I am in charge of rinsing and where, as a baby, I sat splashing on Saturday nights as my mother bathed me.

Afterward we move to the front room to join my father, who sits in his easy chair by the coal stove reading a thick book, and my brother, who runs the train beneath the Christmas tree. Eddie drops a white pill in the engine's smokestack to produce puffs of locomotive steam, and we fight to sound the whistle as Mother sits with legs outstretched on the sofa, reading the newspaper.

Soon I follow my father into the kitchen to the radio, a pre-war walnut console that sits on a low metal cabinet by the back-porch door. But all my father can find there is Christmas music and none of the mystery stories we enjoy, and so turns the switch for short wave. We learn that Christmas day has already begun in England and find more Christmas carols.

Weekday mornings as she works in the kitchen, my mother tunes to The Breakfast Club. Saturday mornings my brother and I listen to Big Ed and Sparky, Tom Mix, The Lone Ranger, and Sergeant Preston of the Yukon. We are always eager to send off for Texas Ranger badges, decoder rings, and pictures of our heroes despite our usual disappointment with these trinkets. Such as the Tom Mix belt made of milky white plastic and stamped with red horseshoes and spurs, which we thought would be made of leather. Or the plastic Captain Midnight ring with secret compartment for coded messages that broke within an hour.

But best are the evening shows on Saturdays and Sundays, when my whole family sits at the kitchen table listening to Spike Jones and his band; The Shadow, who can make himself invisible to catch crooks; the spooky stories on The Inner Sanctum; Gangbusters, where cops chase robbers; and Richard Diamond Private Detective. After a while I go so far into the drama, picturing it in my mind, that I don't even see my mother, father, and brother sitting across the table from me.

But now the sacred music coming from England

seems right, for it is a quiet night, made holy by that quietude. I feel warm and secure with my family in our rustic home. I long to linger near my father and so, without a word, I get out the checkerboard and set it between us. I like the feel and smell of the smooth board my father cut from plywood, scored, stained, and varnished, and of the checkers sliced from wooden dowels.

I play well and think I may win because I have taken half my father's dark-stained men and am about to make a king. But then I am offered a man I must take and sit aghast as my father jumps one man after another, circling the board and landing in the kings' row. I see that I will lose again.

Although I can beat most grown-ups at checkers and have been doing so since I was two, I seldom if ever beat my father. But it's good that he never lets me win, since it would be a hollow victory. I am not so stupid at the game not to notice deliberate misplay. Besides, I am good enough to beat my mother, my brother, and unsuspecting adults whom I lure into games.

One of the adults I always beat and who always comes back for more—delighted by my skill, as if witnessing a dog perform tricks—is Henry Kreminski, my father's boyhood friend. Henry comes in his blue Dodge coupe with his wife Kathryn and their son Johnny.

While the men go fishing in the boat, the women chat and drink iced tea in the shade and we kids play cowboys.

Henry is also of Polish descent but more northern Slavic-looking—round-faced, blue-eyed, and fair-haired—and with a brighter outlook than my father's. In all things Henry is an optimist, and when they return from fishing and start drinking beer on the boat dock, he states his faith in God, the government, and happy endings.

This always gets my father's goat. "That anyone, especially a fellow Pole and descendant of Copernicus, could be so shit-headed naive..." So their arguments always begin, more or less.

Their debates about life-after-death, the New Deal, Eisenhower, and the love of women always grow into heated blue battles that send their wives, Johnny, and Eddie fleeing, but delight me no end. My father's cynicism—always voiced in measured if profane tones and backed by facts gleaned from the thick books he reads—turns Henry's face crimson, raises his voice an octave, and squeezes out of him barked Polish curses I seek to mimic. I also strive to copy my father's debating tactics—the impatient rolling of the eyes, the calm logic and sarcasm—that, I find, only make things worse when I use them on my mother and schoolteacher.

Though I am drawn to Henry's high-spirits and romanticism, in my eyes my father always wins the arguments. Eventually he will be proven right about the myth of happy endings, at least for him and Henry.

But now I sit staring at the checkerboard trying to fathom what happened, bottom lip pushed out in disappointment. My father reaches over, grabs me under either arm, and hoists me into the air—lifts me flying over the checkerboard and lands me in his lap. Both of us now are smiling.

"You had me there for a while, Son. I guess I got lucky."

"You knew all along," I say, but I also believe in my father's luck, which I know I will inherit. Though I cannot foresee that it is about to run out and that this inheritance will for long years be delayed.

His thick, gymnast's arms feel warm and strong on me, arms that worked the rings at the Polish Falcon Hall and pulled him into boxcars as he moved about looking for work during the Depression, that sawed trees in Oregon and broke rock in Minnesota. But soon he will stop using his strong arms, and that will be the end of his best luck.

On this night, Christmas Eve, I have a cold intimation of what is to come. I recall again the earlier conversation in the tavern, that our home stands in jeopardy if my father does not find a nearby job. Despite his warm embrace, the sudden thought of it chills me. I feel I must do something to help save our home.

IX

The home where I long to remain is not a real house, just a converted clubhouse, previously someone's week-end fishing shack. High above it I see silver airliners crossing, headed to Chicago, New York, or Los Angeles. But we live nowhere, on a flat, seemingly endless plain, on a dead-end road in sparsely populated Midwest backwaters.

And under-populated for a reason. It's a place where hardly anyone wants to live. Here there are no stores, restaurants, or movie houses, except miles away in Granite City, a dingy steel town. No sewer, water, or natural-gas lines. Here there is little to do.

Also, the home itself is not suitable for many Americans. Covered in fake-brick tarpaper, it has small rooms and no furnace or central heat, just mammoth iron coal-stoves in the living room and on the back porch. A bottled-gas space heater warms the bathroom, and the kitchen range helps take off the chill when bread is baking. To help keep us cool in summer we have one oscillating fan. During heat waves we eat dinner in the backyard under the tall maple to escape the kitchen, and my parents and brother come sleep with me on the back porch on army cots.

We do have running water, but it comes from a well and is not suitable for drinking. So when my father goes to town he brings home large glass jugs of city water that he fills from a hose at the gas station. Nor is the well water that good for bathing, for in it soap does not bubble.

Electricity was added to the house at some point, and the jerry-rigged wiring is not so good. Time and again my father has to squeeze under the house in the dark, spidery crawlspace to fix it. Same with the plumbing. In fact, something always needs fixing. Doors rot off hinges, windows warp and stick, dead limbs damage the roof. Paint peels from doors, windows, and gutters. But since my father stopped going to the steel mill and has more time, the place looks pretty good. Though in the front room above the kitchen doorway is a line where two shades of rose-colored paint meet. My parents economized and bought only one gallon, then had to go back to the hardware store to have them mix another quart, which didn't quite match.

Other inconveniences about the home would keep most people from wanting to live there. Like the gray laundry room attached to the garage behind the coal bin. Before I started school, I would play make-believe there on cold, rainy Mondays by the black electric space-heater as my mother washed, rinsed, and wrung the clothes. She has big galvanized tubs on legs for soaking and rinsing, and a wringer washing-machine—a white metal barrel with twisting agitator inside and rubber rollers on top to squeeze the clothes through. It takes most of the day to do the laundry and hang it outside on the clotheslines—unless it's raining or freezing. Then it has to be hung on the back porch where I sleep, and on Tuesday mornings I'll sometimes wake in a forest of half-frozen trousers.

On top of that there's the garden to tend, leaves to rake, grass to cut, trash to burn, and garbage to bury. The boat, too, needs constant caulking and care. The dock once collapsed when Homer was standing at the end fishing, so all the men from the city—Homer, Herb, Henry, and Mitty—came to help my father rebuild it, working from the boat.

Also the numerous snakes, spiders, and mosquitoes might deter some people from living there, though these pose problems only in summer.

Although there are no stores nearby, we can get bread and milk at Sis's tavern. Most everything else has to be got in Granite City, even if we need just a piece of sandpaper or an aspirin. Mitchell, population 200, is only a mile up the lake, but no direct road runs there from my home, only railroad tracks near the dead end. Occasionally we do walk the tracks to Mitchell, watchful for trains, snakes, and hoboes, but there's no grocery or hardware store there anyway. Since, like most families, we have only one car (which is sufficient, since my mother does not drive), we learn to plan ahead, make do, and do without.

But living nowhere and knowing little of the outside world makes going to school in Mitchell, Illinois, an adventure, for it sits on Route 66, a conduit to that world. This is By-Pass 66, the route taken by truckers and travelers who don't want to drive congested St. Louis streets. The main road from Chicago to L.A., in 1953 it's just a two-lane highway on which traffic creeps through towns like Mitchell at fifteen miles per hour in the school zone and pauses at the town's lone stop sign.

At noon recess when the weather's fair I go to the school's front gate to watch the passing tractor-trailer trucks, tank trucks, milk trucks, and farm trucks loaded with pigs and cows. And, best of all, olive-drab army trucks carrying smiling soldiers and pulling cannon, headed west, perhaps all the way to California. From the west come dusty sedans with canvas water-bags hanging from their bumpers and weary families peering from the windows, both car and occupants looking tired and defeated.

As I watch this stream of traffic, I dream of Oklahoma oil fields and Texas ranches with wild horses, of Indian villages and endless deserts. All my dreams lie west, and I wish someday to travel that road in that direction, to travel far from nowhere. But not yet. I love living on

Long Lake, with its warm fish and dark mystery.

Fed by numerous springs, the water is always cool, even in summer. And, because the lake barely stirs, it freezes quickly in winter. It is home to frogs, soft-shelled turtles, crawfish, water snakes, and copperheads. Mosquitoes, mayflies, and dragonflies breed on its surface. Sunfish, crappie, and bass; channel cats, mudcats, and carp; buffalo and gar swim in its depths.

In summer, chartreuse-colored moss grows along its shores, where crawfish hide. Then I sweep the moss onto the bank with a garden rake and fall to all fours in the black mud to grab a flopping crawdad from the wet weeds and drop it in a tin can before it can retreat into the water. At times great islands of moss appear on the lake's surface like pale-green glaciers, gliding ever so slowly from the south toward Mitchell, and the fishing is ruined for days.

But the fishing is usually good right off our new dock. The old one collapsed on a Sunday afternoon, when my father's best friend Homer and his family dropped by. We were all gathered in the shade of the tree-lined bank, with Homer out on the end of the dock, cane pole in hand. We heard a loud crack, and half the old slats splashed into the lake. Homer had to edge back to shore along the remaining beam like a tightrope walker.

The dock is a good place to try if you want sunfish

RICK SKWIOT

to eat, as I always do, for they are the best tasting, the firm, white flesh marbled with minute blue veins. Sometimes I can get crappie off the end of the dock and to the left a little, out about ten feet, where my father sunk a Christmas tree. But better is across the lake by the farmer's cows, where cottonwoods stand tall and snow down puffy white seeds come spring. There, in the branches of a fallen cottonwood, lies a good crappie bed. But I can get there only if my father takes me over in his boat, since I am forbidden to take the boat out alone.

Though I did once, my brother claims, when I was two-years-old. He told my mother, and she ran screaming to the neighbor down the lake, old Mr. Rhodes, because I had drifted his way. He got in his own boat and towed me back to shore. But this is all hearsay since I was too young to remember it.

The underground waters that feed the lake are most everywhere. So it's no tough task to sink a pipe and bring up water with a long-handled pump, like the Suttons have mounted on their kitchen sink. But beneath my house lies a small earthen cellar my father dug, where he's installed an electric pump and water heater. So we can just turn on the faucet in the bathroom and get hot well-water pouring right into the tub and don't have to heat it on the stove like the Suttons and Grandma Ida do.

78

I know about the underground water for a fact, because I saw it with my own eyes when Mr. Gray dug his cesspool. He dug it out with a spade, in his backyard up the road, all through June and July. He got down so far that he had to use a ladder to climb in and out, and a pulley and washtub to haul out the dirt. When he got that deep, he struck an underground stream. I could see it when I looked down into the hole, running clear in a small cave.

I figured that was bad luck, and Mr. Gray would have to dig another hole. For maybe it was the same spring that their well drew from, and it wouldn't do to flush your toilet down into it. But that's exactly what Mr. Gray did. A dump truck came with broken concrete blocks and other porous trash to fill in the hole but leave spaces for sewage. Then he put dirt on top and planted grass seed, and that was his cesspool.

Since that day, whenever I step into the lake and feel a cold spring on my legs or take a bath in water pumped from our well, I wonder whether it's coming from the same underground river that runs to the Gray's cesspool, and whether we are upstream or down.

X

At eight o'clock it's time for bed. I wash my hands and face, pull on my flannel pajamas, and, after stoking the back-porch stove, slide into bed. There I find my stuffed dog Blackie, whom my mother made from left-over scraps of her black dress to resemble my lost dog Trixie. Perhaps I would be a happier, less pensive, and less brooding six-year-old if I had not lost Trixie when I was four.

Trixie was a black, curly-haired spaniel, a pup that my father brought home for me. It quickly became my link to the world of animal feeling. I could communicate to him with words and signs, and Trixie would understand. In turn, I could understand the dog's postures—its wants, its sadnesses, its joys.

But one winter day Trixie followed my mother and brother to the crossroads, where they went to catch the bus into town. They told Trixie to go home but the dog stayed. Then they got on the bus.

I sat at the front window day after day, looking up the black tar road, waiting for Trixie to reappear. I left my post only when called to the table but then ate little and returned quickly to the living room sofa, where I knelt staring west.

But now I am warm in bed and content enough with Blackie as my mother comes to me storybook in hand. Since it's Christmas Eve she wants to read to me of the birth of the Christ Child from *The Storybook Life of Jesus*, which she cherishes so. But I shake my head.

"Please read me 'Jack and the Beanstalk.'"

"Not again."

"'Jack and the Beanstalk.' Please."

"I read you that last night. I read it to you every night. Tonight you get this."

I don't like it but realize it's no use complaining further. Thus she reads to me of the peaceful Holy Family in the manger and the birth of Jesus Christ. But I much prefer the tales she has been reading to me for years—'Hansel and Gretel,' 'Chicken Little,' 'Puss in Boots,' 'Little Red Riding Hood,' and 'Jack and the Beanstalk'—stories where boys and girls get threatened by giants, wolves, and witches, where bad people fall to earth dead or get cooked alive, stories with magic and heroes.

My mother tucks me in, kisses my forehead, and turns out the light. However, I cannot sleep—not for any excitement about Santa's arrival but because I get thinking about my father not having a job and our having to move away from the lake, the plum trees, the garden, and the rabbits. I like awake for what seems like hours and finally decide to leave a note for Santa, thinking he might be able to help.

I slide my feet from under the blankets and into my slippers. I scoot across the cold, painted, Masonite floor to the table where my father arranged a drawing board for me after I broke my wrist on Veteran's Day.

By moonlight I take up a fat pencil with soft black lead, grip it tightly, and, at the center of a clean sheet of drawing paper, print:

Dear Santa,

Please bring my father a new job, I don't want to move.

Richard

I fold the note and seal it with a piece of cellophane tape. On the outside I print, "To Santa Claus," and carry it to the darkened front room. There I slide it under a gingerbread man on the cookie plate my mother has put out for Santa and return to the porch to touch my rabbit's foot.

Christmas Day

XI

I am awakened from a beautiful dream of cowboys and wild horses by my brother's high-pitched voice:

"It's Christmas! It's Christmas!"

This is one day when Eddie gets up before me, eager to open his gifts, which he can't do until everyone else rises and gathers round the tree. But I have less interest in the gifts than in the food and fellowship of Christmas that come later.

The muffled songs of screeching jays and chirping cardinals sound from beyond the frosted windows. But instead of rising to race to the Christmas tree as my brother has already done, I lie in bed keeping warm and anticipating the coming day. It's a holiday, the best of days, each holiday with its own entrancing rituals.

I think of the red-and-green wrapped gifts lying under the tree, the drive across the river and into the city, and the exotic aromas of my grandmothers' homes. I visualize the downtown store windows, the evening party at Maria and Claudia's, and the dark ride home nestled in my mother's lap.

This holiday makes me think of other holidays and festivities—of Thanksgiving and the ducks my father shot for our meal, of Easter and the fun of dying eggs,

85

and of Labor Day, which, I decide, is my favorite holiday of all, when fruits are ripe and the weather always warm.

On that day I'm awakened by summer sunlight coming through the back-porch screens and falling across my bed. Birdsong penetrates the screens as well, clear and startling. Now I do not linger in bed but jump up, pull on my blue jeans, rainbow-striped tee-shirt, rainbow-striped socks, and black PF Flyers. I rush out through the screen door, which slaps closed behind me on its long spring, and past the sky-blue morning-glories twining up the trellis.

In the gravel drive sit Herb's blue DeSoto and Mitty's ivory Dodge, and I fear I have risen too late. I race to the white picket-fence that guards the lake and gaze dejected down to the empty dock. The boat is gone, the men already out on the water.

My father always promises me—each Labor Day, Memorial Day, and Fourth of July, when my parents' city friends come for a country picnic—that I can go fishing with the men if I wake early enough to catch the boat. But I never do.

I march alone down the steep wooden stairs to the dock and look both right and left but without seeing a soul on the lake. I take my cane pole from its pegs under the dock, find a small crawfish in the moss along the shore, and bait my hook. I sit on the end of the dock, feet dangling toward the water, awaiting my father and hoping to catch something big to show the men.

Within minutes I see the blue boat come around the bend in the lake, moving silently over still, sun-glistened water, my father in an old bowling-shirt at the oars, Mitty shirtless in the bow with his fly rod broken down, Herb aft, beer can in hand. When I turn back I cannot find my cork and, panicked, yank on my pole but too late. My hook is clean.

Herb and Mitty. Homer, Henry, and Frank will arrive later. As will Vanita, Florence, Bernice, Eula, and Elvira. These names, artifacts of another era, fit their bearers like old gabardine shirts and soft cashmere sweaters.

I kneel on the dock as the boat comes alongside. "Can I see?"

My father hefts from the boat's slats and onto the dock a wire basket holding a dozen thick sunfish bigger than a man's hand, four larger crappie, and three bass—two-pounders, at least. I reach into the basket to touch the fish, to feel their warm, slick bodies, to brush their feathery fins, to inhale their mossy lake-smell and stare into their eyes, frightened eyes, as if they sense their fate. For in minutes they will be beheaded and gutted and by noon lying on the grill.

As the men hack away standing at the rustic, blood-stained table on the lakeshore, I join in the slaughter, scaling a bass as I sit on the dock, the translucent flakes flying up and settling on my hands, my arms, my nose. The last tickles and, hands coated in fish-slime, I wrinkle my nose and try to blow it away with a puff, but without success.

Herb reaches over with a bloody, fish-gut hand. "Here, Rickey, I'll get it."

I pull away, reflexively wiping my own hand across my face and smearing it with fish-slime.

The men laugh as I fall mute and redden. But it is a fine silence and a smiling embarrassment I feel at their teasing, which will continue at spurts throughout the day as they lure me on absurd errands and ask me trick questions. I know they are testing me and teaching me. And though as yet I pass few tests, I pass enough to make me feel a part of their manly circle.

And manly it is to my mind. It's Labor Day, and these are men who work with their hands, union men, whose muscled arms glisten with perspiration when they cast a lure, pitch horseshoes, or raise beer bottles around the barbecue pit.

Soon Homer will arrive in his Buick coupe, Joe in his pointy-nosed Studebaker, and Frank in his copper-colored Nash, each with grocery bags, beer, wives, and children. But for me their cars define them more than their families, as if emblems of their essence.

Homer's sleek green Buick with its deep, throaty growl, plush seats, and smooth, effortless ride, seems to echo his easy-going, soft-spoken, and confident air. In fact, Homer is so easy-going that he just laughed when, as a three-year-old, I filled-in the Buick's chrome portholes with mud.

Uncle Harry's heavyset drinking-buddy Wolf drives a yellow Cadillac coupe with its gas cap hidden under the taillight. Like Wolf, who wears black knit shirts and yellow slacks, it is a fat, lumbering thing. And when Wolf and my uncle leave for California to look for work with no suitcases but a trunk-load of canned beer, I see that the Cadillac is much like Wolf himself.

Even my father's pre-war Plymouth seems just right for him. Unadorned yet handsome, sleek, and happy-looking, with a grill that seems to smile, it resembles more than anything else the dented black lunch-bucket my father carried to the steel mill before he got laid-off.

The men will be dressed in cotton slacks and cool shirts, the women in bright cotton dresses—pink, aqua, or sky blue. Starched dresses are the norm even for casual occasions, as at school, where girls are permitted no slacks. Although at times, when weeding the garden or cutting the grass on hot summer days, my mother will wear calf-length pedal-pushers. But these instances are rare.

My family of first- and second generation Americans dresses more formally than our rural neighbors do. In the family photo-album is a picture of my dead Polish grandfather—also a steelworker—sitting on the grass at a picnic in dress slacks, white shirt, and knotted black tie. And a snapshot of my own father on a name-less lakeshore holding a cane pole and wearing white flannel slacks, dress shirt, and tie. In public, my Ger-man grandmother, Ida, always wears a long black coat and black hat except on the hottest days, and I have never seen the arms of my Polish grandmother, Mary, who covers them in all weather within prim, pressed dresses. Both women always wear black, laced shoes with two-inch heels, even at home.

On Sundays I am dressed in store-bought clothes—starched white shirt, blue suit, and tie—which enforces a certain decorum. If we go visiting straight from church, I am stuck with it, and cannot wrestle in the grass, rum-mage through trash, or dig in the dirt all day.

The somber clothes—generally black, gray, dark blue, or brown—seem to have a similar effect on the adults. In public they are soft-spoken, polite, and cor-rect. They wait their turn, beg pardon frequently, and address strangers as "Sir" or "Ma'am." They always say "Thank you" for the slightest service, even if their due. I am schooled to do likewise and to avert my eyes at another's misfortune and never to stare. In all, I am taught not to draw attention to myself, a lesson that becomes so ingrained that I can never do so in any obvious way, and so learn to become crafty at it.

While the men gather round the brick barbecue with their beer bottles and their horseshoes telling veiled stories I cannot grasp, the women move rustling between the kitchen and the garden or the linen-covered card tables set in the shade of the great maple by the lake. I go to the garden to help the women pick tomatoes and corn, cucumbers and lettuce, and to the peach tree, raspberry bushes, and watermelon patch. The women smell of flowers and huddle whispering, occasionally laughing quietly and shooing me away, telling me to go play or sending me back to the men. There exists an adult world of whispers, signs, and secrets of which I know nothing but ache to learn.

The women carry to the table platters of sliced red tomatoes, bowls of greens, and cream-colored potato salad. From the fire the men bring the browned fish and meat. As I fold my hands and close my eyes in a prayer of thanksgiving, the fragrances of food and sweet perfume come to me on a September breeze.

After the meal, in the hot, late afternoon, we will spread quilts on the front-yard grass to lounge in the sycamore shade, the St. Louis Cardinals' baseball game playing softly on a radio in the window, the weeping willows barely whispering. Conversation is muted, rare. My mother spies in the puffy clouds a polar bear and cubs. Homer encourages me to drink from his beer bottle, which makes my eyes water, screws up my face, and again amuses the men.

Labor Day afternoon reminds me of Sunday, always a day of rest, where you sit quietly looking at clouds, or lie in the hammock reading a book, or play cards, but nothing more, except, perhaps, drive to town for a movie.

Late in the day as the light softens, cicadas begin to call and fireflies appear, which, with the other children, I chase and try to capture. One sits pulsing on my palm. A brilliant yellow flash breaks the dark…

*

But this is not that warm September day, but a cold Christmas morning. I finally rise, slip my feet into fleece-lined slippers, and find my wool robe. I shake the grate on the back-porch stove and shovel in more coal. Then, before joining my brother beneath the Christmas tree, I go to the window.

With the cuff of my robe I scratch through the frost to peer outside to the backyard. There blue jays peck at stale bread my mother threw out the previous evening. But, as I expected since forewarned, Santa did not tether a pony to the maple tree. Nor is there any sign of my father's new job, though I'm unsure what that sign might be.

I am confused about Santa Claus and Christmas

presents. I hear much talk about the spirit of Christmas, the joy of giving, and Santa's jolly generosity. But then, when I visit him at the department store and ask for a pony, the old man's first response is, "Well, have you been a good boy?" My mother also promotes this seeming heresy, that gifts do not spring from any innate desire to please on the part of Santa, but rather are guarded rewards bartered for good behavior.

Also there's the gnawing question of Santa's existence. My belief in Santa is buoyed by having received a typed letter from him postmarked "North Pole" and by the reassurances of my mother, my father, and other authorities—like the minister and the newspaper, sources who claim to revere truth—that Santa Claus is not a hoax.

On the other hand, the worldly eighth-grade boys who sit in the back of the school bus have told me that Santa is malarkey. But after weighing the evidence I discount their word, as these are the same boys who told me there's a killer shark in the lake and far-fetched tales of how babies are made.

While we wait for our parents to rise, my brother and I examine the wrapped boxes under the tree, careful not to touch or shake any, as instructed. But I soon grow bored with studying the colored packages and go instead to the Christmas cards Scotch-taped to the bookcase, which my mother has made into a fireplace for

Christmas, with white mortar painted onto red-brown crepe-paper bricks, and black, gold, and red construction-paper suggesting hearth, irons, and fire. Once again I read the names of the senders and imagine myself in the winter scenes depicted: riding in horse-drawn sleighs, hiking through snowy woods, or sitting before a real fireplace with burning logs instead of one just made of paper.

My mother finally emerges from their bedroom, and my father soon follows. She heats milk for my Ovaltine, prepares a plate of cookies, and pours two cups of coffee from the percolator on the stovetop. It is black, bitter stuff that I cannot abide, even with a stream of Pet Milk poured in. Nonetheless I love the smell of it and the Pet Evaporated Milk can with the calf pictured sticking its head out of a can of Pet Milk that has an even smaller calf pictured in a smaller can of Pet Milk, and so on.

Finally my family goes to the tree to open our presents. I am happy with the cardboard circus that Santa has left for me, which I get to fold and assemble—the big top, the barred wagons with tigers inside, the tiny wooden trapeze on strings. Still, I look about for some indication from Santa, some sort of reply to my note, but find none.

XII

We load the roast goose and the gifts into the car, check the gas range and lights one last time, and leave our home for our trek to the city without bothering to lock the doors. And not just because there's little inside worth stealing. (Besides, the back door won't lock.)

Likewise, in town my father leaves his car keys in the ignition with the windows down, knowing that the car and anything inside it will be there when we return. No one bothers to lock up bicycles either because no one ever steals one. We can also leave our milk-and-butter money in an empty milk bottle on the front porch and no one will touch it except the milkman. Same at school, where I keep my ice-cream money in my desk and no one ever thinks of taking it, since stealing is wrong and getting caught means reform school, I'm led to believe.

It seems you can trust most people with most anything, even in St. Louis. My mother will ask strangers in the department store to watch me and her packages while she goes to the ladies' room. However, I am ordered not talk to strangers nor accept candy or rides from them.

My mother, though, does accept rides from strangers, or at least did once. One evening we got stranded in Granite City with Mabel Sutton and her kids when we went to see *Peter Pan* and *Bear Country* at the Washington Theater. After the movie we found that all the buses going out to the crossroads had stopped running after dark the month before, and we couldn't afford a taxi. A teenager who overheard us on the street said he'd take us all home in his old Chevy for fifty cents, and would have if he hadn't had a flat tire a half-mile from the crossroads.

My parents have no trouble finding an honest and responsible baby-sitter either. Dickie Sutton, who has just turned twelve and thus is considered an adult, will do it for a dollar. But he is far stricter than my parents, not even allowing Eddie and me to draw chalk circles on the carpet for marbles. So if my parents go out dancing at night, they don't have to worry or check on him—which they can't do anyway since there's no phone.

But now my family motors away from our unlocked home, away from the lake and past the crossroads. A mile further on, the tar road meets the concrete highway and railroad tracks, where huffing steam locomotives shake the earth. There sits a roadhouse, The White Swan. My eyes fix on it as we pass, as if drawn there by a magnet.

On top of the low building nests a white neon bird

that blinks off and on at night. A white-stone, fortress-like facade guards it, signaling to me the alluring blue darkness that lies within. I have been inside only once, with my father, who swore me to secrecy on the fact—which makes the blue darkness even more seductive.

It was a Saturday morning the previous spring. I had ridden with him into Granite City, where we went to the hardware store to buy seed and sandpaper. On the way back we skirted the railroad tracks and turned as always toward the crossroads. But then my father abruptly braked and veered the car onto the gravel parking lot of the White Swan, where a lone car sat.

From warming April sunlight we pushed through a padded blue door into a dim yet sparkling blue cave that smelled of sweet liquor and perfume…A low, midnight-blue ceiling with sparse, white Christmas-tree lights looking like stars…Shining metal chairs with dark-blue vinyl seats, and blue-topped chrome tables…To the left, a small bandstand where shining silver drums and cymbals sat…Ahead stood a silver bar with barstools that matched the blue chairs…Perched on a stool where the bar curved I saw a woman in a white dress, a woman with flowing platinum hair and sparkling white teeth, a woman more beautiful than any movie star, and I knew that she was the White Swan.

When my father moved toward her at the bar she smiled, held out a pale white arm with silver bracelets to take my father's thick, dark hand. "Hello, Ed," she said in a throaty-voiced way I had never heard my mother speak to him.

She patted my head and bent toward me with red-painted lips. The perfume scent came stronger now and enveloped me like a white feather pillow.

"You're a chip off the old block, aren't you?"

I nodded speechless.

My father sat on the barstool next to hers. I climbed up beside him. But instead of drinking a beer in a brown bottle as he did at Sis's tavern, he got a clear, icy drink with gin. So instead of my usual I.B.C. Root Beer, which came in a brown bottle like my father's beer, I ordered a 7UP from the baldheaded bartender, who poured it silver and bubbling over ice.

I sat sipping my icy drink in this dark ice palace, the palace of the White Swan, who whispered to my father and who was the most beautiful creature I had ever seen.

When we stepped back out into the sunlight I squinted and felt my father's arm on my shoulder.

"This is man stuff, Rickey," he said. "Something we don't talk about to your mother."

I pressed my lips together and nodded compliance, leaning into my father.

For the rest of the drive home I got to sit on his lap and steer the old Plymouth, though with help from him at the crossroads. I felt myself fill with a solid sense of coming manhood. I knew that I was being schooled as a special son, a chip off the old block.

*

As a six-year-old I understand that just as there is "man stuff," certain things pertain only to women. I never doubt that men and women are different creatures.

On my father's desk sits a bronze paper-weight replica of the Statue of Liberty, and I always note her resemblance to my mother: the same soft features and calm, mysterious expression; the same full figure and staunch posture. But for me my mother represents the opposite of liberty, as do most women—grandmothers, school teachers, church ladies, and neighbor ladies.

Thanks to the petty demands and punishments I suffer at their hands, I have grown wary of them. For it's women who make me wear starched collars on Sundays and mouth stupidities in a dank church basement. Who force me to sit quietly for hours in a hard school desk while outside birds sing. Who come flying witch-like out their door waving a broom at you just for nibbling a few grapes from their arbor or peeing off their dock. Likewise it's their daughters who rat on you at school, telling Miss Bush that you put the toad in Judy's desk. It's clear to me that they stand against all good things—all things wild, daring, and free.

But while the women in my life represent goodness and correct behavior, the men I know are skilled at detouring around it.

From men I have learned all sorts of ways to cut corners, thus saving labor and unnecessary concern about obeying all the rules. With men, easy does it is the rule, and close is okay.

From Earl Sutton—who houses his wife and eight kids in a failed tavern, the long back-bar mirror still fixed to the living-room wall—I learn how to plant a pitch-fork deep in a patch of well-soaked earth and bang it with a sledgehammer so worms vibrate to the surface and you don't have to dig.

Joe Matayas, Gertie's son, whom I visit whenever he's home on leave, teaches me how to polish your boots with cooking oil when you're in a hurry and still pass inspection.

From my father I learn to save the rabbit you accidentally run over, throwing it in the trunk and making up a story about how you trapped it, since Mother won't cook road-kill. My father also teaches me how to concoct tales of flat tires and busted Johnson-rods that made you late, when actually you were sitting in Sis's Tavern drinking beer, playing the jukebox, and talking with Sis's niece from Chicago.

I learn too from old Mr. Joseph, a white-haired gentleman who sometimes comes in a polished Packard to visit my mother, even though he says little. He likes to walk through the garden holding my hand and helping me pick corn or strawberries, and I see what it might be like to have a kindly, good-natured god guiding you, or a grandfather.

I even learn things from red-faced Mr. Lee with his electric paddle, things that have to do with instilling fear and acting like you have horrible punishment awaiting anyone who crosses you, whether you do or not.

I also learn from Pancho, but from a distance and usually in a backwards way. Like the time he shot Wayne in the hand when horsing around with his new shotgun. Or the time he was in the Suttons' backyard varnishing his split-bamboo fly rod that he'd left out in the rain. The Suttons' new beagle puppy came stumbling by and knocked the varnished rod down into the dirt. Pancho leapt up spewing vile words, grabbed the puppy like a football, and threw it against a cottonwood. I, of course, identified with the puppy, which yelped and limped away. So that was a good lesson, which had something to do with innocent mistakes, blind anger, and the Panchos of the world.

Like all boys I am tuned to the signs and symbols of manhood and want more than anything to be able to do and possess all things manly, the things that will make me resemble my father. To have muscled biceps and a beer belly—both of which on shirtless summer days I compare to those of the Sutton boys, though none of us show much sign of either. To carry a shotgun or .22 rifle for rabbit and duck. To own a fly rod and deftly loop the long line back and forth, back and forth in the still air till the feathered fly lands softly on calm water. To possess the dexterity to tie flies that lure fish, to hammer nails true, to saw boards straight. To heft horseshoes and toss them accurately onto distant spikes. To grow black whiskers and strop a razor, to brush your face with cream and scrape it away. To ice-skate, drive a car, wield an ax, and enjoy the bitter taste of beer. To be a hero to some woman. To sit contentedly for hours reading thick books without pictures and smoking cigarettes.

Lucky Strikes are my father's brand, though he sometimes buys Camels, which I prefer for the desert scene with pyramid and camel. I enjoy the click of my father's Zippo, its soft flame, the sound of the crinkling paper set afire, the earthy smell of smoldering tobacco, and the smoke streaming dragon-like from my father's nostrils or, best, floating from his mouth in a series of O's like a skywriter's. Then to have the glowing cigarette dangling from your lip, squinting your left eye as smoke rises to it while you bait your hook or plane a board— this is the epitome of manliness.

XIII

Just beyond the high school lies the street where on Sunday mornings we turn toward Wilson Park and the First Presbyterian Church of Granite City. But today, Christmas, we move past it without a thought, for we are not a particularly religious family. Though I do glance that way, remembering the sliding board at the Wilson Park pool.

Whenever I complain about going to Sunday school, my mother says, "An hour a week is not too much to ask." Although for my father, a lapsed Catholic, it is too much. Each Sunday he drops us at the curb and returns an hour later to retrieve us, never setting foot inside a church, even on Easter.

That one hour a week is the ration God receives from my family, except for our saying grace and my mother occasionally reading Bible stories to me. It's not that my family disrespects the church, God, or Jesus Christ and for that reason bars them from consideration the other 167 hours a week. Rather, the authority of the church—as well as that of the school, the government, or the Scouts—seldom exceeds the authority of the family. Thus my father's testy confrontation with the school principal over my paddling. And the silence at the dinner table—no radio-playing or, later, TV-playing, which might vie for attention.

Still, one gives the church its due: a weekly hour of silent immobility and a dime or two in the collection plate. But for me, like my father, even this seems too much.

On Sunday mornings I'd rather stay with my him, leaving my mother and brother at the Presbyterian Church then going off to do manly things for an hour—like shoot ducks at nearby Horseshoe Lake or have eggs, coffee, and cigarettes at the diner. But I must wait another eight years for this privilege—until I learn my catechism, am confirmed into the church, and thus satisfy my mother, so I can then quit attending.

But for now it is a chore to dress in suit and tie and sit indoors reciting prayers, singing childish songs—"Yes, Jesus loves me, Yes, Jesus loves me"—and being forced to memorize baffling Bible passages.

In my Sunday school class I study my classmates' tight-shut eyes, clenched hands, and beseeching lips as they pray to God the Father. But I hold little fear of this Father Who Art In Heaven, who, compared to the woods, waters, winds, and fields that rule my life, seems so distant and disinterested.

The church itself does its best to drive me away by casting me in an embarrassing Christmas skit dressed as a Wise Man and other attempts to use us kids to amuse adults. One Sunday they march my class down the aisle to the front of the main chapel to join the adult service. The minister, a kindly white-haired man with a red nose, comes from his pulpit to an easel set before the pews. There he takes a charcoal and draws the face of the Devil—a scowling, wicked fellow. But then he turns the large white tablet upside-down, and the Devil is miraculously transformed into an angel, his pitchfork becoming wings and his frown a beatific smile. The other children gawk in amazement. I turn in my pew to see the congregation smiling like people watching the chimpanzee show at the Saint Louis Zoo. I stare back with a bored expression to show I am not so easily gulled, but everyone just keeps smiling.

We cross railroad tracks and motor toward the center of town. The black Plymouth hums past the Tri-City Grocery, where on Saturdays we buy food for the week. Though with fish from the lake, trapped rabbits, and shotgunned ducks, with potatoes, carrots, and onions from the root cellar, and beans and peas in Mason jars in the pantry, we seldom fill more than a grocery bag. At the meat counter Mother usually orders a bone for Monday's soup, scraps of veal and beef she'll grind for meatloaf, liver for liver-and-onions or kidneys for kidney stew, and a chicken to fricassee or fry. At times there is also beef tongue or, on Sundays, Wiener schnitzel. Also stuffed cabbage, pierogi, or meatballs-and-spaghetti. I do not know the taste of steak and lamb-chops, and think stewed offal, simmered soup bones, and braised oxtails superior fare. Soon, however, when we move to the suburbs and I go to the homes of schoolmates, where people eat tuna casserole, frozen pie, and TV dinners, I will come to understand how truly privileged I am.

We pass the hospital, St. Elizabeth's, where my tonsils were removed and my bones set. Reflexively I reach for my left wrist, which still feels weak, since the cast has just come off.

I broke it on Veteran's Day, when my father drove us past Horseshoe Lake to Monks Mound, a hundred-foot-high earthen pyramid built by Mississippian Indians a thousand years ago, then the largest manmade structure north of the great Mexican Pyramid of the Sun at Teotihuacán. A chill gray November day but a fine day for a picnic breakfast, according to my father, who set-up the kerosene camp-stove on a picnic table for Mother to brew coffee and fry bacon and eggs.

After breakfast, while playing with my brother, I fell from a tree, my wrist bending awkwardly beneath me.

At St. Elizabeth's I was wheeled on a gurney into a basement operating room. A white-veiled nun in a long, white smock came sliding across the polished floor to me, placed a wire mesh over my face, and poured on ether. I tried to kick and scream and run from it, but instead was dragged into a cartoon-like dream of a col-

106

orful boat on bright seas, into a false, celluloid world. I felt as if I was dying, being torn from life, and fought it sensing that nothing imagined or make-believe could compare to this world of chill gray mornings, rough-trunked trees, and broken bones.

I returned from the hospital with the cast on my arm knowing I would not be able to climb trees, wrestle, or roughhouse for weeks. But I found that my father had constructed a drawing board for me, mounted it on a homemade lectern, and placed it on a card table by the back porch window where the carrot and sweet-potato plants grew. Before it he had positioned a worn barstool and on the board had thumbtacked sheets of rough drawing paper. Beside it lay rows of colored pencils and charcoals.

There I spent long November and December hours concocting great battle scenes with airplanes, tanks, and submarines—gray ones with the red-white-and-blue American star and green ones with the Red star. I also drew landscapes of dark-green forests and rushing blue streams like the one on the lighted Stag Beer sign at Sis's Tavern.

Soon we pass the steel mill, sitting like a great yawning monster, with its clanking railroad cars, mounds of coal, smoking chimneys, and gaseous smell. The factory both attracts and frightens me, and makes me feel awe for my father, who had helped run it.

He had worked as an inspector on the night shift, which to my mind was good, for then days we were together. While my brother was off at school I was at my father's side, watching. Not often asking questions but listening to what was offered as instruction or humor and watching, watching his hands.

Hammering, sawing, planing. Digging, plowing, planting. Tying flies, rowing across the still lake, feeding waxed line onto the water from the thin, green reel, and cutting the sky with the long, looping line.

It's the same with my mother. I am forever watching her fingers: kneading dough, peeling carrots, shelling peas. Knitting a sweater or lap robe, darning a sock over a wooden egg. I particularly watch her hands when she sews—measuring and cutting cloth, pinning tissue patterns to her dressmaker's dummy Lulu Belle, threading one of her many colored bobbins into her electric sewing machine—her one prized possession—and feeding the fabric past the hammering needle that threatens her fingers. Not the rough, thick fingers of my father, but thin, soft, feeling fingers.

Their hands smooth my hair, caress my cheek, toss me in the air, and always catch me. But these are hands I also fear when I am willful and wild, particularly those of my father. But that is only right and just, and I accept my punishment as fair price to pay for my misbehavior.

Even now, as an adult, I can sense his hands on me,

just as I can smell his skin and feel the black stubble of his chin harsh against my face. I see his hands, as square and strong as he himself, hands at work. I can see too how he became less himself and less a man when he no longer used his hands and his heart in his work.

Steel is honest work. Work that his father did before him, which allowed Joseph to come to America, have a bride sent to him from his village, and begin a family. And so too with the son. For steel is honest work when you're pulling hot brick or pouring castings for the wheels of locomotives, the tracks of tanks to face the Panzers, or the girders of growing buildings.

But a salesman—which he was soon to become—does not use his hands so much. And though my father's suits always fit him well and made him appear more successful than he ever was, he never again looked comfortable. And even if what he sold was worthy—and he convinced himself that an insurance policy was a worthwhile thing to sell to a working man without a dime in the bank who needed to pay his funeral expenses and provide for his family—it killed something in him to do it, to repress his innate shyness and quietude and coax folks into buying. Not using his hands broke his heart, which finally gave out when he was sixty-one.

It was shortly before his death, before he went cold-blue after drinking his last highball and dancing a polka with his wife, that I came to spend a few days with them after vagabonding across Europe. On a winter morning he and I walked up the suburban street where they then lived to the shopping center, for coffee at the new McDonald's. As we pushed through the steamy door, a young woman with painted face, clown suit, and balloons tied to her wrist approached to hand us each a coupon. My father kept his hands in his coat pockets, shook his head sympathetically, and said:

"Whatever they're paying you, honey, it ain't enough."

For years I thought it just another example of his cynical humor. But now I see that he shook his head not in sympathy but in empathy, that he was talking not about her but about himself, speaking from experience.

XIV

We continue on, moving over a vast viaduct with scores of railroad tracks beneath, and through Madison and Venice, Illinois, two more factory towns.

I recognize the place where, on my weekly trips to St. Louis with my mother, we change from the bus to a streetcar that climbs a trestle and rocks us over the Mississippi River. The track then bends, the old flat-end car with its musty, brocade seats leaning over rusty scrapyards on the Missouri side. Nose pressed against the glass I feel my stomach rising and await our sudden, dark descent into the comforting tunnel that takes us under St. Louis skyscrapers to the 12th Street Station.

But today we ride in the black Plymouth with its itchy wool seats, rumbling across the McKinley Bridge, streetcar tracks down its center where the wheels of the Plymouth slip from side to side. We stop at the toll booth on the west bank to pay our dime and turn south toward downtown St. Louis, or The Mound City, as it is called, after Mississippian Indian mounds that once lined the river.

Grandma Mary lives by a small park with a baseball diamond and a fountain where, in summertime, children bathe. But on Christmas morning the air hangs clear and cold and the park stands empty.

My father kills the engine and without a word slides from behind the steering wheel. He moves across the herringbone brick sidewalk in his wine-colored letter-jacket and disappears into a narrow, sunless walkway between two redbrick buildings.

The rest of us remain in the car. I gaze up the street to the poultry shop on the corner, where geese, chickens, ducks, and turkeys stand waiting in metal cages for the white-bearded man with the blood-smeared apron, who reminds me of God as depicted in *The Storybook Life of Jesus.*

After some minutes my father returns, opens the car door for my mother, and releases my brother and me from the back seat. Together we march in file down the dank brick passageway between the buildings and mount the stairs in back, shoes hammering the wooden steps.

I no longer question this routine of waiting in the car, having done so once before and gotten a perhaps plausible if vague reply from my mother: "Your father needs to talk to Grandma Mary alone. We'll go up soon."

Only decades later—when my mother is facing death (just as she faced life, with good cheer and resignation) and no longer has reason for secrets—do I learn the truth. My father precedes us upstairs to chase away the man who shares Grandma Mary's bed and whose existence is hidden from us children for propriety's sake.

Now I think warmly of this poor man, whoever he was. Likely a Polish immigrant like Grandma Mary, who, after forty years in America, spoke no noticeable English. I think of him on Christmas morning being rousted from the widow's warm bed, or maybe rushing through his hot breakfast, taking a last gulp of steaming coffee before being sent out into the cold.

Where can he go? What could be open on Christmas morning 1953 other than a church or precinct house? Even drugstores and gas stations close on holidays and Sundays. Today there is no newspaper. It is a holy day, kept holy by most everyone keeping quiet and staying put.

I see this nameless man, my grandmother's lover, shivering as he descends the backstairs, walking hands-in-pockets across the treeless backyard, shuffling over the cold cobblestones of the alley, a hand-rolled cigarette in his lips, muttering Polish curses.

Maybe he has a friend he thinks to visit. But it would have to be a good friend to receive him empty-handed on Christmas morning, when most families are gathered around the tree exchanging gifts. So I see him roaming the streets, looking wistfully through tenement windows at warm hearths and lighted trees, and repeatedly passing by the watch-repair shop on North Market Street to glance at the clock in the window.

Stepping into Grandma Mary's flat I cross into an

exotic world spiced with the odd sounds of her Slavic tongue and the familiar aromas of steaming kiska, warm Russian rye, and frying Polish ham.

She stands at the center of the shining, linoleum-covered kitchen floor not five feet tall, gaunt and silver-haired, in a prim gray gabardine dress, white lace handkerchief peeking from her pocket. The facial resemblance to my father (and ultimately to myself) always impresses me. Though I do not yet understand procreation and all that it entails, I can see that she is my father's mother and I my father's son. But while the strong jaw, deep-set eyes, prominent nose, and fine black hair make my father a handsome man, similar features in her make for an overly masculine and homely woman.

These are not northern Slavic features. No fair-haired, round-faced, blue-eyed Poles in this family. But dark, wolfish folks, perhaps descendants of raiders from the East. Or of Gypsies, for that is the look and the temperament: dark, taciturn, and suspicious; wary of institutions and the larger civic order; nomadic. Or perhaps descendants of the Neuri, militant Iranian nomads who inhabited Eastern Poland in the Fifth Century B.C. and who, according to Herodotus, turned into wolves at certain times of the year.

Today when I read of recently urbanized nomads who, after a few months of setting up home on a street in, say, Riyadh, will fold their tents and move across the street to another, identical plot of sand, when I read of these nomads I think of Grandma Mary. She seemed to relocate annually to an identical second-story shotgun flat with polished hardwood floors, checked linoleum in the kitchen, and mothballs in the closets, each apartment within a block or two of the poultry shop. I know I share those nomadic instincts and blood, whether Gypsy, Neuri, or Hun.

The rich Slavic tones, a mix of soft vowels and harsh diphthongs, come to me—though mostly in the words of my father. Even in her native tongue Mary is not talky, and my father is forever lecturing her and throwing up his hands in frustration over some stubbornness or another that neither I nor anyone else in the family can divine.

Polish is my father's first tongue as well, spoken at home and, at the time, on Cass Avenue, where immigrant Poles gathered in the early 1900's. Spoken too in the National Catholic Church, Piekutowski's sausage shop, the bakery, and the bars.

The foreign mother-tongue is both a curse and a blessing to my father, who views his ethnicity as the social handicap it truly was in his youth and early manhood. So he refuses to teach Polish to my brother and me, whom he thinks will thus better blend into the dominant Anglo culture. But he does not have the forethought or the heart to anglicize our name from Skwiot to, say, Scott.

But the blessing of the foreign mother-tongue is that he did not learn English until beginning public school, and then from rigorous and well-spoken English teachers instead of from parents and peers. As a result his English is grammatically precise, slang-free, and unaccented, his voice deep and commanding. To hear him speak you would think him a university-schooled radio announcer. It's what makes others think he would be a good salesman.

But Grandma Mary's English is another thing entirely. She takes a tentative step toward Eddie and me and presses a white envelope on each of us.

"Mahree Creezmos."

Most everything else she has to say to us boys or to my mother must be translated by my father, who after a while grows exasperated with much of it and refuses to translate.

"What did she say, Dad?"

"Naah, you don't need to know."

Mahree Creezmos.

But I do remember this much of what she said: the story she once told me of her childhood, in a village near Zawady, Poland, before World War I. I can't recall how much she actually spoke and I actually understood, how much might have been sign language, how much my father might have translated, or how much I may have embellished it with my own imagination. I wrote about it once in a short story:

> *Although it was a cloudless summer day, Maria and Kristina looked to the sky when they heard the rumbling sound, as if searching for thunderclouds. Then they realized their mistake.*
>
> *They ran over the mud road of their village toward the safety of Kristina's cottage. Maria, a lithe twelve-year-old, reached the cottage before Kristina, who was slowed by her infant, Piotr, at her breast.*
>
> *As Maria pushed through the plank door, she turned to see the only image she would ever dream of her native land for the next seventy years: Kristina on her knees, breast naked, mouth open but mute, gaping at the Cossack galloping away with Piotr hanging limp from the end of his saber.*

Then, when she was seventeen, her family somehow arranged her passage to America. Within a year she married my grandfather, Joseph, who was forty-five and from the same Polish town—but who had left for America two years after Mary was born. I suspect it was an arranged marriage of some sort.

Obviously life was vastly different and very difficult then and there for Mary, Joseph, and their kin. Which makes me reserve judgment of her and those involved in her migration, with the exception of the Cossacks. I see that my grandmother likely had her reasons for being mute, rigid, and wary, for never touching me.

But now it is Christmas morning and this is America, and I have an envelope with a new dollar bill in it and a Christmas card signed, simply, "Skwiot." At the kitchen table she places before me a plate with the fried Polish ham on Russian rye-bread and a piece of steaming kiska—a heavenly sausage of blood, liver, and buckwheat groats spiced with hot pepper—alongside a fried egg. It is breakfast, and we all dig in.

There's little talk around the table except for brief and acrimonious exchanges in Polish between my father and grandmother. But the mood is bright, and the sharpness in their conversation is expected and not bothersome, as if a necessary ingredient in their close and emotionally charged relationship, like pepper in the kiska. We're a quiet family, who can enjoy our food and the pleasure of our own company without need to comment upon it. For me, eating kiska with eggs and watching my strange-bird of a grandmother sitting in her best dress drinking beer from a can at nine o'clock on Christmas morning is great fun.

My father winks at me and I nod back, acknowledging tacitly our shared appreciation of the rare food, which is nothing like the canned stews and soggy carrots served in my school's cafeteria. I understand that this is a privilege, a good, secret thing that few people know about and appreciate.

I know mine is a privileged and enchanted life, and that I have the unqualified alms and affection of the dark, handsome man and the quietly smiling and beautiful, fair-haired woman across the table. I know that later that night, after all the food and gifts, relatives and fun, they will wrap me in a scratchy blanket and carry me sleeping to the black Plymouth and then, at journey's end, put me to bed on the back porch that faces the frozen lake, with flames from the coal stove dancing in silhouette on the wall, like fairies.

XV

Though I know mine is a privileged existence, I do not understand how truly beneficent and rare it is. As with most children of my day, my experience is limited largely to my own family. As a result, I think all families are more or less like mine. Mine is normal, I think, albeit a cut above others, for my father has told me so.

I do not think it odd to have a grandmother who cannot speak English, nor to draw chalk circles on the living room carpet for marble games. Nor to shake a coal grate on cold winter mornings to get warm, to pick corn from the garden for the evening meal, to cull sunfish from the lake in order to eat. I am, I'm sure, a normal boy.

When I come to see families who live in endless suburban tracts without lakes or fruit trees, who eat dinner in shifts, whose mother is gone from home all day, and who fight bitterly among themselves, I think such families abnormal, even after my own becomes such a family.

But I already have bitter and angry people in my life.Chief among them is Pancho, a stocky, brush-haired thirteen-year-old who lives up the road a mile and rides past our house standing on the seat of his motor scooter arms spread Christ-like. He terrorizes us younger boys by throwing firecrackers at us, dropping chicken dung on our heads, and shouting out angry blue curses when playing horseshoes with Raymond Sutton. He pelts stray dogs with stones.

Pancho lives with his grandparents, who lavish gifts upon him, like the split-bamboo fly rod that he left outside in the rain, the Harley-Davidson scooter on which he flies down the road, and, for his birthday, the double-barrel 12-gauge shotgun that he shot Wayne Protter with. On the school bus I study Wayne's hand, now forever curled uselessly, and think fearfully of Pancho.

Then there is the man down the road, Mr. Gray, who hates dogs because a stray once dug up his tomato plants. One winter morning when chasing rabbits with the Suttons, I found a dog shot dead in the night, lying stiff in the ditch across from the Gray home. Eventually Mr. Gray strings an electric fence around his garden to protect it, but succeeds in killing only his daughter's pet spaniel.

Also there is Mr. Nolan, who lives on the lake at the road's dead end and who backed his Ford over Charlie Washburn's legs the previous 4th of July after drinking all day.

Just across the road from the Nolans live the bespectacled Nazarene preacher, his pale and sickly wife, their skinny four-year-old daughter, and their overgrown and obnoxious son, Glenn. One bright summer morning—with the help of Russell and Roger Sutton—I tried to hang him from an apple tree in his front yard and failed only because Glenn's mother came outside and chased us away.

But we saw the execution as necessary and right. Glenn, who is bigger and stronger than the rest of us, had gotten a lasso for his birthday and went around the neighborhood practicing calf roping and such on us smaller boys. After a week we all looked like escaped galley slaves, with dark-brown rope burns on our wrists, ankles, and necks. That's when, in self-defense, we hatched the plot to hang him.

Afterward, his mother walked up the road with her daughter and stood on the front porch telling my mother that I was a killer. This made Mother cry all afternoon and send me to stand in the corner.

"Wait...just wait till your father gets home!"

But my father did not overreact so. When I told him how the Suttons and I had lured Glenn out of his house with false promises of making up, then jumped him, hog-tied him, and began hoisting him into the apple tree at the end of his own rope, I saw a glint of pride in my father's eye. However, for my mother's benefit I had to be spanked, which my father did with no great enthusiasm but at length, for I refused to say I was sorry.

XVI

Grandma Ida lives but blocks away from Grandma Mary, on North 14th Street. We make the short drive on largely deserted cobblestone streets bound by redbrick tenements. While either grandmother is forbidding to me in her own way, it is Grandma Ida, the sour German Protestant, who most repels and scares me.

At Grandma Ida's an inhibiting tension always hovers in the air and grows tauter and tauter as the day grows longer. Whatever affection she may hold for me is tempered by a wariness, as if waiting for me to break a vase, spill my milk, sass my parents, or somehow misbehave. When such inevitably occurs, Grandma Ida is the first to condemn and correct me. Perhaps she sees something of her husband in me.

She and Uncle Harry, who sleeps on an army cot in her front room between marriages, are both silent, distrustful sorts. Not until much later do I understand that their silence and distrust—actually a distrust of words and thus of thought—likely lie in intellectual dimness.

Certainly my attitude toward them is influenced by the example of my father—who, conversely, is well spoken, humorous, and playful despite his mercurial Slavic soul and the funks it sometimes produces—as well as my father's assessment of his in-laws. Once, when I was three and being carried in his arms down the dark backstairs from Grandma Ida's and Uncle Harry's flat, I felt his breath in my ear.

"Thank God, Rickey," he whispered, "that at least you can choose your friends."

But this is the last Christmas we will share with Grandma Ida, who will die in June. My mother is to learn of her death when she visits her in the hospital after a minor illness and finds her bed empty. When she asks a passing nurse about her mother, the nurse, without pausing replies, "Oh, she's dead."

That nurse's comment still hangs like a black cloud over my family history, reminding me why I was so repelled my slow-eyed German kinfolk: They were nonentities. People who could be casually and disrespectfully dismissed, even in death. And worse, who confirmed and accepted their low status with a sullen slavishness.

Emerging from the Plymouth I inhale a steamy cloud of St. Louis sewer gas rising from beneath the city through the storm drain on the corner. It's an unmistakable odor of dark crevices and decay. The smell seems to permeate the red bricks defining this world: the redbrick streets, the redbrick herringbone sidewalks, the two-story redbrick tenements standing cheek by jowl down both sides of the block.

We move through another dark, musty, brick-enclosed walkway to the backyard, where a line of green-painted outhouses sit at the alley's edge. Although this is the United States of America, the richest nation ever known, and although this is the civilized core of one of its most populous cities with downtown skyscrapers not a ten-minute walk away, and although this is the second half of the Twentieth Century and the Romans had indoor plumbing two thousand years earlier, Grandma Ida still does not.

Rather, she lives in an antebellum coldwater flat with one lone faucet of chill water in the kitchen sink. A handsome but archaic Greek Revival building with jerry-rigged wiring added after Edison, it also houses genera-tion upon generation of indigenous American mice de-spite baited mousetraps under Grandma Ida's bed and the living room sofa, where I occasionally spend the night. The mousetraps sometimes crack me from sleep, like death clapping in the night.

But notwithstanding the outhouse, lone faucet, mice, and second-hand furniture, I do not think my grand-mother poor, though poor she is. For me her home only means a chance to explore—to examine dead mice, search the attic for relics, and linger in the glass-flecked alley behind the outhouse, which I scour for odd beer-bottle caps to add to my collection.

But by most all other standards Grandma Ida is poor

and raised her children—my mother and my Uncle Harry—in poverty. Both of them were taken from school at age twelve and placed in jobs to help relieve that burden.

Although now as dour, silent, and homely as Grandma Mary, Grandma Ida was once a beautiful, straw-haired young woman, the daughter of German immigrants. She married a rakish and charming musician and dance instructor, Emil, who ran a dance studio in North St. Louis, at the corner of Easton and Kingshighway.

By 1919 they have two young children, not yet in school. While Ida already knows about Emil's weakness for the jug, this year she discovers his weakness of the flesh. She learns (how, we do not know) that he is having sex with his female students. (However, we do know that Ida once sends her five-year-old daughter to fetch her father from a tavern, and the girl reports back that he has a woman on his lap.)

But whatever she learns and however she learns it, Ida takes the extreme measure, in 1919, of divorcing her husband and refusing even one dime from him to help support her children. (Anyway, he would drink himself to death within a few short years, so any help she might have accepted would likely have been feeble and certainly temporary.) It is a time when women of her station do not divorce, for such a young woman cannot easily earn a living wage, much less support a family, and there is no government subsidy to encourage such independence.

So she goes to work as a live-in domestic at the German Children's Home while her own children sleep in the dormitory at the orphanage and are permitted to visit their mother for a few hours on Sundays. Such is divorce American-style circa 1920.

Some seventy-five years after the event, while researching family history, I find that the 1920 census lists my grandmother's residence as the State Mental Hospital on Arsenal Street and her occupation as "inmate." When I tell my aged mother of my discovery, she stares off for a few seconds, nods, and says, "Oh, yes. I remember Aunt Lennie saying Mom was having trouble with her nerves and that I would stay with her a while."

But soon Ida leaves the mental hospital and goes to work as a housemaid for well-heeled South St. Louis kin and eventually establishes her family in the cold-water flat on North 14th Street. And although it is a mean life—they often can afford no milk, no meat, no Christmas presents—it is not an unhappy one, by her daughter's accounts. They can still afford to laugh—at their plight if nothing else—and find neighbors and lifelong friends who are hardly better off than they and with whom they sit on the front stoop evenings and sing, which costs nothing.

But now, after enduring Grandma Ida's embrace and

but a minute of the warm, cloying kitchen atmosphere, I rush again outside, where the sharp chill on my cheeks and fresh, cold air in my lungs pleases me. Down the wooden stairs to the backyard—this also covered in red brick. There I scout the coal chute that descends to the cellar, examine the incinerator next to the outhouse, and go to the alley to comb for treasure.

The alley is an alluring place. Although vendors sometime come down the street in front pushing their carts and selling vegetables, ice cream, or hot tamales, and people still sometimes sit on front stoops talking to neighbors or singing, the alley holds more secrets and more life.

In the alley on gray winter days you can see families in their lighted kitchens cooking, kissing, or fighting. You see them carrying out their garbage or running to the outhouse. And while the fronts of homes here all look pretty much the same—the same aged red bricks, the same swept sidewalk, the same sheer curtains—from the back you get a better idea of a family's nature by noting the state of their garden, the number of whiskey bottles in their trash, and the color and condition of their underwear on the clothesline.

The alley is also where, in summer, the men drink beer and play bottle caps, trying to hit a swirling and curving pitched beer-bottle cap with a broomstick.

I search for treasure there but rather gingerly, since I am wearing good clothes. Not my combat boots, worn trousers, and bomber's coat, but brown wool slacks and dark-green corduroy shirt (both sewn by my mother), the brown dress-shoes I wear to church, and a gray, hound's-tooth overcoat that was once my brother's.

Nonetheless I find two mills—the plastic coins that people used for money during the war—one green and one red, a Miller High Life bottle cap with the leggy blonde I secretly love sitting on a crescent moon, and a playing card, the King of Clubs, which I sense is good luck, for it resembles a four-leaf clover. I slide it into my pants pocket alongside my rabbit's foot, knowing luck is a good thing to have. But even if you are born with it as I was, I understand that you can lose it if you don't guard it. So I am forever touching my rabbit's foot, knocking on wood, and saying secret prayers to the gods that govern catching fish, winning at checkers, and shooting marbles.

Now I hear my mother calling—"Richard! O, Richard!"—and run back down the alley and up the gray-painted stairs to the second-floor flat.

Inside more gifts are exchanged. I share with my brother a leather football from Uncle Harry. From Grandma Ida we each receive an apple, an orange, and a red-net bag of walnuts—much the same as we got from the skinny, beer-breathed Santa at the Pontoon Beach VFW Christmas Party.

I want to return outdoors to play football even

though I do not know the rules and can barely grip the ball. But I am told I have been outside in the cold enough already. Besides, the bricks will scuff the new ball. So while my mother helps Grandma Ida in the kitchen and my father and Uncle Harry drink beer and smoke in the front room, Eddie and I construct domino homes and long, curving files of domino soldiers that we fight to knock down.

Uncle Harry fetches photographs of himself in Paris, which I have seen before: Astride his motorcycle in dark wool overcoat and white M.P.'s helmet. Posing in front of the Eiffel Tower. Standing guard against German saboteurs before an elegant building with ornate, wrought-iron balconies, which I believe is Army Headquarters. Only years later do I learn from Uncle Harry that he is in fact guarding an officer's brothel, to keep out enlisted men.

Soon we ring the table in the stuffy, good-smelling kitchen and say grace in unison, the two women standing behind their chairs. Mother lifts the roast goose stuffed with sauerkraut onto the table. The sharp smell of the kraut and the thick aroma of browned goose-fat enfold me like warm, scratchy wool. There are mashed potatoes and canned peas, cranberry sauce, and finally pumpkin pie with whipped cream. Excellent fare, to my palate, excepting the peas, which I try to hide under a pile of goose bones. My parents catch me at this ruse but, since it's Christmas, give me dispensation, and this once I can leave the table without cleaning my plate.

Beside the kitchen cupboard stands a gray door. When my father goes to the front room to smoke and my mother and grandmother are at the stove heating water to wash and rinse the dishes (or "warsh and wrench" on Grandma Ida's Teutonic tongue), I pry it open and slip through.

Behind the door lies more grayness: dingy stairs that I mount soundlessly and that lead up to a colorless attic with grimy windows and gray slat floor. Gray dust-motes hang in cold, musty air, cold as a grave. Gray dust lies everywhere, a century's worth of indifference coating everything like a thin, gray blanket.

In the center of the floor sits a gray tin washtub and corrugated-iron scrub-board. Each Thursday the women boil water on the kitchen stove and carry it steaming up the stairs. I see my mother on her knees, bent over the tin tub, fists working a garment up and down the scrub-board as if grating cheese. Above, on crisscrossed clothes-lines where the laundry is draped on rainy days, a few gray sheets and pillowcases still hang.

The colorless, airless attic smelling of neglect depresses and frightens me. But it lures me as well, for I know that here in this grim room treasure also lies. I steal toward it, toward the coffin-like steamer-trunk beneath the fly-specked window. My eyes are drawn up to the window momentarily by the cooing of pigeons, which I spy on the black-tar roof.

I lift the lid of the trunk slowly, as if fearful of releasing ghosts, and start when I see the arms and legs of Uncle Harry's army uniform resting there. Beneath the uniform in a shiny black-metal sheath lies a dagger with a swastika on its hilt. I slide it from its sheath with a tinkling, scraping noise that sends a ripple up my spine, and lay it across my palm to examine it for blood.

I discover more treasure: a tintype photograph of a young woman in a pleated dress buttoned up to her chin, wispy blonde hair curled atop her head. Grandma Ida on her wedding day, I have been told, but find it hard to believe. Grandma Ida is a heavyset, heavy-jowled woman with stringy gray hair and sad gaze, who ambles about uneasily on thick legs, and this is a slender young woman with a hopeful smile, a straight back, and vivid, dancing eyes.

My mother's voice comes lilting up the stairs: "Are you up there, Rickey? Come down or you'll get dirty. We still have to go to Maria's."

I close the heavy trunk-lid, careful not to catch my fingers, brush dust from the knees of my trousers, and rush from the grayness back downstairs into the warm, bright kitchen, eager to wash my hands under the cold kitchen tap, to rinse from them the feel of death.

XVII

By the time we bid Grandma Ida goodbye and march single file down the back stairs, stars hang in a black sky. But in December the sun sets in late afternoon, and the better, freer part of the day, in my eyes, lies before us.

Now once again in the backseat of the Plymouth I can see my breath in the still air as the old car moves shaking over cobblestone streets. My father swings the large black steering wheel to the left, guiding the sedan onto a smooth, wide boulevard. A streetcar passes, bell clanging, its interior lit ivory in the night.

The city is dark even downtown, so dark at night. The low, bulbous street lamps produce only feeble yellow light, above which a black sky presses close. We move past great buildings that disappear into the blackness, looming like staunch gray sentries over the city.

Soon my father pulls the car to the curb at a building with brightly lit windows, and I stand craning my neck to see over the front seat. I recognize the Famous-Barr Department Store, where each Christmas we stop to gaze through the windows at some elaborate and fanciful Alpine scene in miniature, with toy trains chugging about. It is a ritual.

There are many such rituals in my life. Stoking the coal stove and checking the rabbit traps on cold mornings. On bright, summer morns picking dewy strawberries or raspberries for my cereal. Harvesting apples in fall. Checking for the first sprouts of spring. Drawing the shades at sunset. Simple, peasant rituals that produce a fundamental happiness in me.

But this urban ritual fortifies me as well. I press my nose to the department-store glass to watch the crossing-gate drop as a steam locomotive races by, the mechanical guard sliding from his shack, glowing red lantern in hand. Although a country boy at heart, I spend one day each week on city streets and treasure the city for its unique smells, its machines, its throngs of varied people.

Thursdays after school my mother, brother and I take the bus to Granite City and catch the streetcar that carries us over the river to St. Louis and deposits us beneath the Globe-Democrat Building. (On these trips my mother carries at the ready in her lapel a three-inch-long hatpin, her weapon of choice since her days as a downtown shop girl). From 12th Street Station it's a short walk to Grandma Ida's flat on North 14th Street, where the two women do laundry on the attic scrub-board while we boys play in the alley.

But in summers when there is no school, we leave for the city early in the morning and make a day of it, including an excursion downtown to Union Market and the department store, or to nearby Biddle Market.

The markets hold me in awe, for food is never far from my mind. There are greengrocers with polished fruits and vegetables stacked high, the rich-smelling cheese counter, the butcher with calves' heads, oxtails, and pigs' feet. But the fishmonger is my favorite, with fish schooling in a sea of ice and looking still alive. When the man behind the counter turns his back, I reach up to brush the rough scales of a buffalo with my fingers or touch a dead sole's eye to see if it will blink.

The buffalo fish look so good to eat—like enormous bass. Once, as the fish man wraps a pair of smoked whiting for my mother, I ask if we can eat a buffalo fish for dinner.

She frowns, pats my head, and bends to whisper, "No, sweetie. Those are for colored."

I follow her gaze to a black man at the far end of the low counter selecting a gutted fish.

Negroes, as they are called—or, even more delicately, colored—add to the exoticness of the city. There are only whites in the country and at my school, except for the lone Mexican boy in my first grade class, who lives with his mother and little sister in the old crossing-guard shack in Mitchell.

But at downtown markets colored are all about, piling in and out of service cars—long DeSoto limousines painted chartreuse and black—since even taxis are segregated. At Sportsman's Park, where my father takes me to see the Browns or Cardinals play, we sit in a grand-stand of white faces, for colored are relegated to the right-field pavilion. Nor do I see a Negro at any soda fountain or cafeteria where my mother might take me. When we go on "the boat," the Admiral, which cruises the Mississippi with a dance band in the ballroom for adults and a penny arcade on the lower deck for kids, we do so in the company of other white passengers. Colored are allowed only on Wednesday evenings.

Although my parents accept the prevailing apart-heid as given, they do not tolerate racial slurs and de-mand from me respect for others, whatever their color, and the common courtesy they believe is everyone's due. However, such courtesy, from whatever quarter, has its limits, I later learn, since a colored man cannot join a trade union, or a colored woman give birth at the best hospital, or a colored child attend the school in the next block if it is reserved for whites.

However, the word "white" doesn't seem to fit my family—at least not my father and me, who are a long way from colorless and whose skin is nothing like the pink "flesh" crayon in my Crayola box. In summer, when my father works shirtless in the garden and paddles the boat bare-chested over the lake, he grows darker and darker in the sun, so dark that his fair-skinned wife feels uncomfortable being seen with him in public. This for fear that others might think she's with a colored man and thus abuse them.

But for me the varied people pleasantly pepper the city, adding even more spice to what already is so piquant and colorful...The dime store with its rainbow of straw cowboy-hats hanging over the toy department; the hardware store with creaking slat floors, rough nail-kegs, and acrid aromas of metal and paint; the soapy-smelling yard-goods floor of the department store, where I pick out the wool plaid my mother sews into a shirt; the sweet-air soda fountain where on hot summer days I sit on a rotating metal stool, bare legs dangling, sipping on a root-beer float; the red streetcars clanging and great trucks smoking; the cop on the corner with his blue uniform, white gloves, and piercing silver whistle; the legless man on a rolling wooden platform and the sharp-nosed blind man with black glasses and tin cup into which my mother always drops a nickel; the Ambassador Theater, with its red velvet seats and roaring lion at the film's start, from which I hide my eyes; the chrome-and-glass Forum Cafeteria, where on Mother's Day I eat strawberry shortcake; the department store Santa Claus with fake beard and rubber boots on whose lap I sit the Friday after Thanksgiving; the employee cafeteria atop the Famous-Barr building, where everyone eats standing up because there are no chairs; the fire station we always pass, with polished pole, smiling men in blue, and gleaming red engine; the feel of hard bricks and broken glass beneath my feet and hot sun radiating up my legs. Back on Grandma Ida's block, the dark, rank, spidery outhouse. The tavern on the corner where cigar battleships float on brown spittoon seas and the smell of smoke and stale beer waters my eyes. The barber shop next door with its nutmeg air and slick magazine photos of muddied men at war. On the street men pushing carts and calling "Hot tamales" or "Melon! Cantaloupe!", or grinding knives, or picking through the alley trash. It is all so rich and dizzying but somehow makes my ultimate return to the still lake, rabbit-filled fields, and cool, damp earth ever the more so sweet.

XVIII

The black Plymouth rattles on cold and dark, tires slapping cobblestone streets. I stand in back on the ridged rubber floor looking out the windshield at passing warehouses and two-story flats, all of red-brown brick.

The city stands dark, the neon Budweiser, Michelob, Stag, and Falstaff signs that normally glow on nearly every corner now cold and dead. Few cars ply the streets, even North Broadway. But occasionally I am cheered by a lighted Christmas tree in a window, the bulbs shining red, green, blue, and white. But this gloom punctuated by light and cheer seems appropriate to me, for I am going to the home of the Leonelli sisters, where there are both.

Their home, another two-story brick building, on Tyler Street, stands near North Side factories, including John Deere Tractor, where Maria, the older of the two sisters, works as a secretary. It's a neighborhood where you can walk to the factory, the church, the market, the bar. Maria and Claudia will continue to live there long after their father dies and their neighbors move away, and will not leave until the old brick building next door collapses onto theirs.

From the cold car and the dark, quiet street I follow my mother into a warm, bright-lit parlor filled with high-pitched voices and music. The two sisters, Maria and Claudia—followed by their married sister, Theresa—come from the kitchen to hug my mother and press warm, dark faces to mine, faces nearly as dark as my own father's in summer.

In the family photo-album is a picture of the three Leonelli sisters with my fair, teenage mother, who looks like a lily among dusky roses. The photo dates from days when other German, Anglo, and Irish children were often forbidden to play with these dark-skinned intruders into their city. But it was different with my mother's family. They were even poorer than Italians. And the Leonelli family—which lived next door and fed my mother when there was little to eat, taught her to cook Italian, and cared for her like their own—is also her family.

The house is raucous with the sound of phonograph records—a novelty for me, since we have no record player at home—and the screams of Theresa's children coming from the next room.

"Go to the kitchen, Rickey," says Maria. "The kids are making plaster Paris."

I go, but reluctantly despite all the cheer. For these children seem truly foreign. Not because they are Catholic Italians but because they are city kids, and I slip among them like the shy country mouse I am.

Though always cordial toward me, the two brothers and their sister never really bother to size me up as I do them, as if not taking me seriously. Also, they are louder, more talkative, and fidgety. They are always playing records, yelling at each other, complaining, or having the radio going in the background. Theirs is a noisy, demanding family, of which I am happily not a member. Importantly, the boys do not play marbles and hardly ever go outdoors to the alley or street, especially when it's cold. They do not climb trees. They seem less interested in the outside world than their own interior worlds and have no names for birds. They are always joking, always clever, and easily hurt. Though unknown to me at the time, they are what I will become later, when I lose touch with my lake, my fields, and my woods.

But I have a second and more important reason why I'm slow to go to the kitchen: the presence of their grandfather, whose wheelchair I glimpse from the living room.

I do not like to go near him or even to be in the same room with him, for something bad and scary comes off the man. He is, I have been told, an invalid, who cannot walk and does not speak. He sits thin and feeble with glazed eyes, his expression never changing from a fearful half-smile.

His two youngest daughters, Maria and Claudia, both now near forty, are good Catholic girls who have always cared for their father, ever since their mother died and their brothers and Theresa married and moved away. They are saints, my mother tells me, for caring for their father, and will always live together and never marry.

So I feel guilty about my fear of their invalid father who has made them saints. That is until years later when my own mother is likewise an invalid in a wheelchair and tells me the story of Mr. Leonelli.

It's a simple story. When his young wife died suddenly, he got a gun and shot himself in the head, so he might join her in heaven. But his aim was not so good, and he left himself only crippled and forever dependent. That is how he sainted his two youngest daughters.

Nonetheless I go to the noisy kitchen where the kids are making plaster-of-Paris figures from rubber molds their aunts bought them for Christmas and painting them with watercolors. But it takes me a while to understand this, that it is their Christmas present they are employing. Already half the paints are gone or spoiled with foreign colors, the encrusted molds strewn about the table and sink, and the cardboard box they came in lying crushed on the floor. It depresses me. Not because it's a more expensive gift than I would ever hope to receive, but because of the way it is being abused and exhausted, as if a gift has no spirit.

I'm glad when I'm called into the living room. Both my brother and I receive miniature John Deere tractors from the Leonelli sisters, and I am happy to push its rubber tires over the hard slat floor, turning the green metal steering wheel and imagining I am plowing a spring furrow in the garden.

I stop and look from my toy tractor to my father, who sits in a cane chair on the far side of the room amid the circle of adults, a highball in hand. Then I turn to the thin, sagging Christmas tree in the corner and ask myself, Could this be the sign from Santa? Will another green but man-sized tractor be awaiting Father at home, so he can be a farmer? Then we could stay at our country home and not have to move to the city and play with city kids.

I touch my rabbit's foot and King of Clubs and knock on the wooden floor, praying that Santa Claus is real, kind, and forgiving, like Jesus, and not just make-believe or vengeful. I pray that I will never have to leave my home.

XIX

I am carried semi-conscious from the Leonelli house to the cold car, where my mother holds me in her lap. I feel her chest heave against me.

The car rumbles over cobblestones then glides over a smooth boulevard, and I feel its tires slip on wet street-car tracks. We stop. My father rolls down the window to pay the bridge fare. Next I hear the tires hum over the metal grid of the bridge, sense the Plymouth descending to the Illinois side, and retreat back into sleep.

When we arrive home I barely wake but feel the damp, icy air from the lake on my face as I am carried to the cold back porch and put to bed under wool blankets and a cotton quilt. I try to stir myself, to rise and see if Santa has brought the green tractor for my father. But I cannot and fall into a dream of rabbits running in the field and blue jays squawking out a warning. But I cannot heed the dream warning of the blue jays and will ultimately wake from my beautiful dream to a living nightmare.

It is a nightmare set on shadeless suburban streets where no birds sing, no ducks fly, no fish jump. Where life comes inside rooms, through antennas, over telephone wires. In it I do not recognize my father, who now dresses in suits, yells at my mother, and strikes me in anger. Nor do I know my mother, who is not in the kitchen baking pies when I get home from school, for she too now goes to a job. Neither do I know myself. I now resist going outside into the unbuffered sun and onto the brown-baked lawn, or, in winter, out into a sterile cold where there are no rabbits and no tribe to hunt with—just contentious and competitive boys who come to accept me not for being myself but for becoming like them. So instead I sit silent in a room I share with my brother, reading of soldiers and cowboys, of trappers and Indians.

At my new school—a modern school with great windows everywhere but no Indian mounds or wheat fields outside to gaze at—I sit at my desk staring out those windows nonetheless. When my teacher tells me to get busy with something while the others finish their lessons, I take out crayons and a piece of newsprint and draw a picture of a boy resting beneath an apple tree with fields, a lake, and a country home in the background. I draw this same picture hundreds of times over the next few years, and then one day finally stop.

But that reality still lies in the future. On this Christmas night I dream only of my Eden, lush and idyllic but unlike the garden in Genesis, of which my mother reads to me from the Bible. Here there is bitter cold, hard work, and loss; here there is grief. Which makes my paradise better than the one in the Bible. For without the dead winter, there would be no startling and restoring spring. Without the work of hauling coal from the icy bin, the fire would not feel so warm and welcome. Without loss, no longing or hope.

Epilogue

Some years ago, long after my father had died, I returned to St. Louis after a sojourn in Mexico. My mother had sold the suburban home where they lived all those years since leaving the lake and taken an apartment downtown.

Since we were both feeling nostalgic I drove her across the river. Up over the old, dilapidated McKinley Bridge, its surface patched and potholed, and down into Venice, Madison, and Granite City. Past ghostly, abandoned steel mills and shuttered shops.

Beyond Granite City, suburbs now extended into what once were wheat fields. We moved past the old crossroads, approached the lake, and then, just as we reached the bend where the lake road straightened toward Lazy Lane, we both felt a premonition and looked at each other. I almost pulled the car to the side of the road and turned it around. I wish I had.

As we moved down the road and gazed at where our rustic home once stood, we saw a charred black shell. Even the trees surrounding it—the old maple in back by the lake, the tall sycamore in front, the plum trees, the apple trees, the peach trees, the willows—had been burnt black.

I thought of my father nailing down roofing tiles

and pushing his hand-plow in the garden, where now an unkempt mobile home sat. I saw my youthful mother planting tulip bulbs by the front steps and leading me on our morning march around the kitchen table. I saw myself on the dock lifting a golden fish from the lake with my cane pole.

We did not linger, and I did not return until recently.

The length of Long Lake is now fully developed, with homes and businesses lining both shores. Silt from agricultural and construction run-off over the years has reduced its depth to a foot and a half in most places. As a result, the lake has lost virtually all its aquatic plant life. There is no moss or crawfish. Few turtles, sunfish, crappie, or bass remain—only some carp and buffalo. The lake is dying.

A Chemetco, Inc. smelting operation north of Mitchell was found to have used a secret pipe to dispose of wastewater contaminated with lead, cadmium, zinc, and other pollutants directly into the lake for ten years, until stopped by the Illinois EPA. Chemetco and four individual defendants pled guilty to felony charges relating to it. Its former president remains a fugitive.

At Mitchell all but one of the four remaining Mississippian Indian mounds were leveled by bulldozers in 1963 to make way for Interstate 270.

In North St. Louis, many of the antebellum redbrick flats of my grandmothers' neighborhood have been boarded up, burned, or razed, though Grandma Ida's flat still stands, albeit in disrepair, amid vacant, rubble-strewn lots, as if miraculously spared in a saturation bombing. Biddle Market is now the City of St. Louis Mosquito and Rat Control headquarters.

The world of my childhood seems largely gone—the world of coal stoves, electric paddles, and seren-dipitous Sunday visits. Of contemplation, quietude, and independence.

Arthur Miller once wrote that the question all drama—and, perhaps, all literature—tries to answer is, How does a man make for himself a home? It is per-haps the central question not just for writers but for everyone. It's a question I've been unable to answer satisfactorily for myself. For my home—the home with the lush garden, ripe fruit, and quiet family in the small boat on the still lake—no longer exists except here, in a haze of memory. Perhaps that is why—in addition to my nomad blood—I have wandered so.

But despite my wanderings, in my heart I will al-ways live at Long Lake. I see myself still kneeling on the sofa watching for my lost dog Trixie, waiting, hop-ing, staring west, as if I will be touched by a miracle, as if with the dog's improbable return all the grief and loss and longing of life will be solaced, replenished, and fulfilled. And after such waiting, when deliverance comes it will first come ambling up the road like a lost puppy, then as an August breeze sweeping rain-cool and corn-sweet across the lake, more cool and sweet and good for its long, long journey and its late arriving, just at the moment you thought to give up hope.

Acknowledgements

I wish to thank the Madison Country (Illinois) Historical Society, the Lovejoy Library at Southern Illinois University at Edwardsville, the Illinois Department of Natural Resources, the Illinois Environmental Protection Agency, the St. Louis Public Library, and the *St. Louis Post-Dispatch* for help in my research for this book.

I also give special thanks to my colleague and friend Tom Rami for his deft readings and perceptive criticism of the manuscript.

A Note About the Author

Rick Skwiot is the author of two novels set in Mexico: *Flesh*, which won the Hemingway First Novel Award, and *Sleeping With Pancho Villa*, which was a finalist for the Willa Cather Prize.